10

P9-DHI-477

The smart cookies' Guide to Making More Dough

The smart cookies'

GUIDE TO

Making More Dough

How Five Young Women Got Smart,

Formed a Money Group, and

Took Control of Their Finances

The **smart cookies** with Jennifer Barrett

DELACORTE PRESS

THE SMART COOKIES' GUIDE TO MAKING MORE DOUGH
A Delacorte Press Book / October 2008

Published by
Bantam Dell
A Division of Random House, Inc.
New York, New York

Book design by Patrice Sheridan

Library of Congress Cataloging-in-Publication Data
The Smart Cookies' guide to making more dough : how five young women got smart, formed a money group, and took control of their finances / The Smart Cookies with Jennifer Barrett.
p.   cm.
Includes bibliographical references.
ISBN 978-0-385-34244-5 (hardcover)
1. Finance, Personal.   2. Investments.   I. Barrett, Jennifer.
II. Smart Cookies Money Group.
HG179.S535 2008
332.024—dc22   2008026468

Printed in the United States of America

www.bantamdell.com

10 9 8 7 6 5 4 3 2 1
BVG

For our moms
(the original **smart cookies**)

Debbie, Miriam, Marg, Sano, and Tina

Acknowledgments

We first want to thank Jean Chatzky. When you suggested that we write a book on our success as a money group, you ignited a spark in us that has been burning bright ever since. We are incredibly appreciative of your support and grateful for your time and guidance.

To Oprah Winfrey: Because of you, we are truly living our best lives. Thank you for inviting us to share our story. You have become such an important advocate for money groups across the country. You exude warmth, positive energy, and purpose. You have forever changed our world, and for that we offer our deepest and most sincere gratitude. You have given us an opportunity to enrich the lives of millions of women, and just as you do, we will strive to help others to shine.

To the amazing and incredibly hardworking team at Harpo—you rock! To say our time with you was more than magical would be an understatement. In particular, we would like to thank Stacy Strazis. You are all good things wrapped up into one beautiful package. We feel blessed by your friendship and grateful for your guidance. Thank you for believing in us and for reminding us to "go with your gut." Your advice during the early stages of our career set the wheels in motion for all that has followed.

To our literary agent, Richard Pine, for your sound advice and intellect. Thank you for keeping us calm and focused during some of the most exciting times! Everything you said would happen did, and much more. You've surrounded us with the best and the brightest and created opportunities for us far beyond our wildest dreams. Our thanks as well to the Inkwell Management team for your continued support.

To the U.S. and Canadian teams at Random House, whose support, enthusiasm, and guidance have been invaluable, including: Irwyn Applebaum, Nita Taublib, Barb Burg, Theresa Zoro, Susan Corcoran, Anne Collins, Susan Traxel, and our fabulous (and patient) editor Danielle Perez.

To our writer and friend, Jennifer Barrett, we couldn't have asked for a better partner. You embody everything that a Smart Cookie should be. You shared our passion and vision for this project from the moment we met and you far exceeded our expectations. Your talent, patience, and easy spirit are more appreciated than you could know. (And to Jennifer's husband, Victor Ozols, who has been a tremendous source of support and encouragement.)

To our group of trusted experts who graciously agreed to review the manuscript, including: Liz Pulliam Weston, David Bach, Jeanne Brutman, Howard Dvorkin, Jane Barrett, and Dan McGinn. We also want to give a special thanks to Miles Goacher, Ed Barrett, and Patricia Williams—bona fide financial experts who are both wonderful models of fiscal responsibility and wonderful parents. Your insights and feedback helped to make this a better book.

To our manager, Justin Sudds, a heartfelt thanks. From the moment we walked into your office, it was clear that you "got" us. You always seem to know when to step in and when to step back (and when we just need some comic relief!). You are a trusted friend and a respected partner in business.

To our much loved group of friends (you know who you are). We count on you to keep us sane, to keep us laughing, and to keep us going. Thank you for your support and your unconditional love. Most important, thank you for being happy for us.

Our biggest thank-you is reserved for our families. When we first came to you and said that we were leaving our full-time, well-paying jobs to pursue a passion, you didn't try to dissuade us. Rather, you hopped onboard and have been encouraging us ever since. Some of our best business ideas have come from you, and we love the phone calls and conversations that begin with "I was thinking about another idea . . ." You are our loudest and proudest cheerleaders. We are sure at times your neighbors, colleagues, friends (and anyone else within earshot!) may be tired of hearing about what the Smart Cookies are up to, but your pride in us swells our hearts. Thank you especially for understanding the time commitments that accompany this incredible journey and for giving us the freedom to chase our dreams. We love you and feel your support every day.

Contents

Foreword

I first met the Smart Cookies on the set of *The Oprah Winfrey Show*. The show was called "This Is Your Year to Get Richer" and it was devoted to wrapping up a year-long series called the Debt Diet, during which three families had undergone massive money makeovers on-camera. I was one of the Debt Diet coaches, working with a family I'm proud to say came through the program with flying colors and continued to soar.

Millions of *Oprah* viewers—as they always do—tuned in. Many joined us in taking the Debt Diet challenge, signing up on *Oprah's* website to track their own progress, download our tools, and recharge their financial batteries. These five young women were among them. They took our Debt Diet as inspiration to start their own money group. They called themselves the Smart Cookies. And when our producers went looking for success stories to feature on the last episode of the series, we found them.

Andrea, Robyn, Katie, Angela, and Sandra were—at the start of the series—a lot like most women. They had five figures of credit-card debt. They weren't earning what they felt like they deserved. They spent more than they made. They felt behind the eight ball where their money was concerned: ashamed, afraid, embarrassed, naive. But unlike most people, they decided to do something about it. And they decided to do that something together. (If you've ever had a running buddy or a diet buddy, you know together is so much better than separate.)

In the chapters that follow, you'll read about their accomplishments and setbacks, their successes and their frustrations. You'll see five financial lives that could have stagnated or spiraled downward but are now on the right course. And you'll see that you have the ability to execute this sort of turn-around too.

What impressed me most about these five women—what inspired me to suggest that they put their experiences down in writing—was that they did this with no Wall Street experience, no MBAs, no hedge-fund-managing boyfriends or spouses. They caught the message that I've been preaching for years: Managing your money is not rocket science. It takes a little bit of work, a little bit of knowledge, and a little bit of willpower. Once you have those things, it's difficult not to succeed.

The other thing that got to me about the Smart Cookies is their ages. "I wish I'd learned this ten years ago!" If there is one regret I hear over and over again—from listeners to my radio show, *Today* show viewers, or *Money* magazine readers—it's this. "Turn back the clock, please, now that I know the miracle of compound interest, now that I know that small amounts of money saved (i.e., not spent) really do add up to big bucks over time."

Andrea, Robyn, Katie, Angela, and Sandra not only got the message. They got the message young. They are living examples of what happens when twenty- and young-thirty-somethings actually do pick up the ball and run with it. Reading their stories may be precisely what Generation Y needs to start doing the same thing itself.

Jean Chatzky
April 2008

Introduction

The Smart Cookies' Story

If you're like most people, you grew up with certain expectations about what life would be like as an adult. You probably assumed that after you graduated, you'd find a job, work hard at it, and move up the metaphorical ladder, steadily increasing your salary as you advanced in your career—just like your parents did. By the time you hit your thirties, you'd have a home, a husband, and maybe a family. There'd be money in the bank, a budding retirement account, and all the trappings of adulthood: annual vacations, jobs with benefits, and a mortgage.

But if you picked up this book, we're guessing that your life doesn't yet match your expectations. Instead of feeling financially secure, you may still find yourself counting the days between paychecks. Although you're several years into your career, you may be struggling just to keep up with what seem like ever-growing monthly expenses, not to mention trying to set some money aside for the future. Even though you're making a decent salary, you're probably using some of it to pay down your credit cards, school loans, or the car you financed. If you missed even one paycheck, you could be in trouble. How are you ever going to save enough for that vacation, much less a home, a baby, or retirement?

Here you are: a smart, successful woman with a good career. So why can't you get ahead financially?

No matter how well-educated you are, unless you majored in finance or business, it's unlikely that you ever had any formal training on how to manage your money. And for all your parents did to prepare you to succeed once you were on your own—giving you food, shelter, clothing, and encouragement when you were young; pushing you to get good grades so you could get into college (which they might have even paid for); and offering "loans," generous gifts, or a place to stay after you graduated—they probably didn't teach you all the financial basics you'd need to truly succeed. They might have tried, offering general advice about spending less than you make or setting aside money in a savings account. But you probably never got the specifics to help you apply those lessons to your life like how to estimate actual living expenses, buy a home, or get rid of credit-card debt while still saving money for your long-term goals. That's where we come in. We want to fill in all those blanks that have kept you from achieving financial success.

We've written this book with women in mind because we are women ourselves and because too often it seems that our gender lacks confidence in our abilities to manage money well. We want to change that. Men are no better with money than women (research has shown that). But even today, it seems there's still an unspoken assumption that men are inherently more capable of making and investing money than women—how many female stockbrokers or financial advisers do you know?—and that discussing finances among women is somehow improper, or at least impolite. In many households, it's still assumed that the husband will be the main breadwinner and that he will handle the finances. The association between men and money has been passed down from generation to generation, just as child care and housekeeping are still considered women's work (even though most women are now holding down a full-time job in addition to their domestic duties). So what happens? Women often cede control of their money to the men in their lives—whether it's a boyfriend, father, or financial adviser—or they are left to figure out their finances on their own by trial and error. Both are potentially costly methods that can put you years behind in reaching your goals and reinforce underlying, if untrue, beliefs that you can't successfully manage your money on your own. Is it any wonder then that so many women our age are doing well in every other area of their lives yet they can't seem to get control of their finances?

The problem isn't that you're *unable* to manage your money; you're just unprepared.

Did you know how much money you'd need to live on your own when you moved out of your parents' house? Had you ever prepared a budget (or spending plan, as we like to call it)? Or set up automatic bill payments online? Or had the faintest idea that—thanks to compounded interest—the "18 percent APR" on your credit card actually added up to more than $18 per year for every $100 you charged? Did you know whether, or by how much, your employer matched your 401(k) contributions or the advantages of opening a Roth IRA? Did you understand what a FICO score was or how important it would be in determining how much you'd pay for everything from car loans to mortgage payments?

If you're shaking your head, don't worry. We may be Smart Cookies now, but we certainly didn't know the answers to most of those questions when we formed our money group. We were just like you: successful women struggling to get control of our finances. At the time, three of us worked together in marketing and public relations at a multinational company. One of us was a social worker, and the fifth worked at a TV production company. Each of us had her own unique money problems, but we all shared a desire to turn our situations around. We just weren't sure where to start.

Then, in early 2006, some of us (who had flexible schedules or TiVo) saw an episode of *The Oprah Winfrey Show* that featured several financial experts offering advice to families on paying down debt. Over the next few days, during conversations with friends and colleagues, we realized that there were others who were looking for a way to improve their finances too. We thought: Why not do it together? In the end, the five of us found one another, through existing friendships or mutual friends, and decided to form a money group—kind of like a book club, but instead of reading and discussing books, we'd be reading our bank statements and discussing ways to pay down our debt and make more money.

We bought almost every book in the personal-finance section of the local bookstore and read through them all, gathering the best tips from each. We sought out mentors and asked how they made and managed their money. We collected months' worth of bank and credit-card statements, bills, and pay stubs—not an easy task!—and made a commitment to be brutally honest about our financial situations and do everything we could to improve them, to support one another, and to keep all conversations from the group meetings confidential. Though we all knew of one another, some of us had never actually met until we formed the group, and none of us had shared our financial problems with the others. The prospect of disclosing our debt and our financial foul-ups was a little scary for all of us at first; that's information we hadn't shared with anyone. But, as we learned in our first meeting, it was partly our reluctance to deal with or to discuss our financial problems that had left us all in pretty bad shape.

Between us, we realized, we had a combined $35,000 in debt and barely any savings. Two of us had recently emerged from long-term relationships, and we had little experience or confidence in managing our own money. Another was engaged and worried that her shopaholic tendencies would put a serious strain on the couple's finances and their impending marriage. Though she made a lot of money for someone her age, she usually spent all of it (or more) before the next paycheck arrived. How was she ever going to save enough to help pay for their wedding, not to mention their long-term goals? Our fourth was in even worse shape. She was drowning in debt, having maxed out a revolving line of credit from her bank as well as two credit cards—one of which had recently gone into collections when she could no longer keep up with her payments. And our remaining money-group member had recently moved out of her parents' house after carefully stashing away nearly $8,000 in savings. But within a year of living on her own, she'd not only blown right through all of that money; she was now accumulating credit-card debt as well.

Needless to say, we were a collective financial mess. Our money problems were affecting every area of our lives: adding stress to our relationships, keeping us up at night, and making us feel less secure about ourselves and our futures.

At the time, it seemed like it would take years of drudgery and deprivation to dig ourselves out from under our debt and start to build real wealth. But, to our surprise, within a year of starting the Smart Cookies Money Group, we'd already made substantial progress—and without sacrificing our social lives, our sanity, or even our Starbucks lattes! Even we were surprised at how much we'd learned, how much we'd accomplished, and how much fun we had doing it.

In just a year and a half, we'd added thousands to our retirement accounts, paid off nearly all of our credit-card debt, saved more than $25,000, and our engaged member and her fiancé even managed to pay for their $22,000 wedding *in cash*. One of us had gone into business for herself, each of us had significantly increased our incomes, and had either bought, or were planning to buy, homes. Barely a year after the *Oprah* episode that inspired our money group aired, we were being featured on her show ourselves, talking about our accomplishments!

We were no longer trying to avoid, deny, or cover up our financial situations. We were celebrating our successes and working toward even bigger goals. We were no longer scared or intimidated at the prospect of handling our finances but excited by it—especially after we'd proven to ourselves that we were not just capable of managing our money but were good at it. We no longer felt suffocated by our debt or trapped in our jobs. We had increased our incomes substantially and paid down our debt. Most important, each of us had taken sizable steps toward achieving the kinds of lives we'd only dreamed about a year earlier.

Now we want to help you do the same. We're not going to lecture you for past mistakes. We've made them ourselves. We're not going to overwhelm you with a lot of financial jargon or big promises. We're simply going to share with you how we did it: the strategies we used, the lessons we learned through our own experiences, and the expertise we've gained through research and interviews with successful, self-made women we've sought out along the way.

We'll explain how to start your own money group, but you don't need to be a part of one in order to take control of your finances now. Our book is designed to provide you with all the information you need to achieve financial success on your own, no matter how much you're earning or the amount of debt you're carrying. But this is more than an instruction manual. When you buy this book, you are joining a community of women who are committed to being financially successful. You can log on to our website (www.smartcookies.com) to stay connected and on course. Use the site to chat with other women going through similar experiences, and download worksheets and additional tools.

In the upcoming chapters, we'll provide you with both advice and support. We'll give you specific exercises to keep you on track and accountable. We'll also share our successes—and our slipups—to inspire you and to remind you that we've been there too. We've made mistakes. But we've also made great progress. And you can too.

We know what you're going through. And we're here to tell you that it is possible not just to turn your financial situation around but to improve every aspect of your life. You truly *can* have it all: the dream job, the dream house, an abundance of money and love. It is well within your power to make it happen. We're going to show you how.

Just by picking up this book, you've already proved that you're a Smart Cookie. You're ready to take control of your finances and transform your life. By the time you finish this book, you will have dramatically changed the way you think about money and you'll start to see improvements in your bank account and in your life. You'll know how to pay off your debt as quickly and painlessly as possible and how to lower the interest that you're paying in the meantime. You'll know how to invest your money in order to get the best returns by *your* deadline. You'll know how to be financially savvy and still be fabulous. You'll know how to save money for big-ticket purchases without feeling deprived and while still having fun in the meantime. You'll know how to increase your income now and how to buy a house that's not just a home but a real moneymaking investment. You'll have a clear picture of the life you want in a year, two years, even five years—and how to get there—and you'll be amazed at how much closer it will seem.

It's time to take control of your finances and start living the life you deserve. Let's get started!

About Us

ROBYN: THE CASH COUNSELOR

When Robyn became a Smart Cookie, she was 31 and working as a social worker at a nonprofit agency, where she made about $42,000 a year. She and her husband had divorced nearly two years earlier, and she was still struggling to get on top of her finances. She'd managed to invest about $3,000. But she'd gone through $16,000 worth of savings after the divorce and now owed $12,000. Her goals were to earn a master's degree and get a better-paying job, buy a bigger home, and pay off her debt. Within a year and a half of joining the money group, she had done all four. She completed her master's degree in social work and increased her earnings by $40,000. She had nearly paid off all of the $12,000 that she'd owed, invested another $4,000, and bought a bigger condominium using the $80,000 profit she made selling her first home. With her social-work background, Robyn became our designated Cash Counselor. She was good at making us feel at ease discussing our finances, and she really understood the psychological reasons behind our spending habits.

ANGELA: THE MONEY MAGNET

Angela was 26 when she became a Smart Cookie and was working long hours at a TV production company for little pay (she earned about $10 an hour and often worked 60 hours a week). She really liked her job, but she had no savings and had just cashed in her retirement fund to help purchase the condo that she shared with her boyfriend of nearly four years. The couple also shared their money, though—as Angela would openly admit to us later—she'd given her boyfriend complete responsibility for their finances. So she had little idea of where their money was going, or what she was entitled to, when the two separated not long after we started meeting and she was suddenly forced to take control of her finances. Her goals: to save more money and to find a new career that she loved that would pay enough to fund her dreams. Within 18 months, she had started her own business, more than doubling her previous salary, and built up more than $8,000 in her savings account. Not only did she increase her paycheck, but she constantly came up with creative ways to save or earn extra money—from selling old clothes on craigslist.org to taking a part-time job at her favorite furniture store so she could take advantage of the deep employee discounts to furnish her home. As our resident Money Magnet, Angela has helped the rest of us come up with new ideas for attracting more money too.

SANDRA: THE SAVVY SPENDER

Sandra was 24 when she became a Smart Cookie. She'd recently moved out on her own and was working as a public-relations coordinator. She owed $2,000 and had run through all the money she'd saved up while living at home. She'd invested a little ($500) in a retirement account but wanted to increase that amount substantially. She also wanted to buy her own condo, move up to become a public-relations manager, and develop smart spending strategies so that she would never go through her savings or carry a balance on her credit card again. Within a year and a half, she landed her job as a PR manager, increasing her earnings by $15,000. With more money coming in and new spending habits in place, she was able to pay off all her credit-card debt, save $4,000 and invest $4,000 more, and was already making plans to buy her first condo. An admitted shopaholic, Sandra has also proven to be a Savvy Spender. She's become adept at scouting out fabulous finds at bargain prices—whether it's trying on a specific brand of jeans in the store and then buying them on eBay instead (where she got them for half the in-store price) or getting more than $900 off the regular price of a beautiful leather couch by finding a "slightly damaged" model that had a tiny, nearly unnoticeable rip on the underside.

ANDREA: THE DEBT BUSTER

When Andrea became a Smart Cookie, she was 28 and working as a marketing manager. She had used the $120,000 profit she made selling her first condo to buy a new one downtown, where she had always wanted to live. But she owed $18,000 between her two credit cards and a credit line she had through her bank, and she had nothing in her savings account. Worse, she'd fallen behind in payments and one credit card had gone into collections. She'd maxed out the other card, plus the credit line, and nearly used up the overdraft protection on her checking account. She wanted to pay off both credit cards and the line of credit she'd gotten from her bank, earn more money at her job or find a better-paying one, and start saving so she had a cushion in case of emergencies and could work toward other long-term goals she wanted to accomplish. Within a year and a half, she had found a new job in marketing as a director and increased her earnings by $20,000, paid off all of her debt (and remained out of debt), saved $3,000, and increased her monthly contributions to her retirement account. As the Smart Cookie who had the most consumer debt—and paid it all off!—Andrea became our official Debt Buster.

KATIE: THE NUMBER CRUNCHER

Katie is our youngest member—just 23 and working as a public-relations manager when she became a Smart Cookie. She owed $3,000 on her credit card and had no savings. She'd been smart enough to invest in a condo with her then-fiancé (now husband). But her compulsive spending was beginning to take a toll on their relationship, and she wanted to make a change before they got married. She also worried about how they were going to pay for their wedding. But within a year and a half, Katie had paid off all of her credit-card debt and increased her salary by $25,000—first, through a promotion at work, then by taking on a number of freelance contracts. She and her husband also saved enough to pay for their $22,000 wedding in cash and still have enough left to pay off the $15,000 they owed on their car loan. Katie also accomplished a lifelong dream of starting her own PR business, which increased her earnings, and her confidence, even more. A whiz at calculations—whether it's comparing the returns on her investments or coming up with a spending plan that will allow her to save more money—Katie is a natural Number Cruncher.

chapter 1

The Taboo Topic

Starting the Conversation about Money

Money.

How often have you said the word aloud? How often do you talk about it with your friends, your family, or your colleagues at work? Do you know your best friend's credit-card balance? Or how much your parents owe on their mortgage? Have you ever asked your colleagues how they manage their money?

Probably not. To do so would seem almost as intrusive as asking about their bedroom activities, right? Or worse! In fact, we're probably more likely to share stories of our sexual exploits than to divulge details about our paychecks or credit-card statements with our friends and family.

Money is ever-present in our lives. We use it daily and can't survive without it, yet women hardly ever talk about it with each other. We've been conditioned to believe that it's impolite to ask how much money someone makes, or how much they paid for their home, and distasteful to disclose how much we earn from our investments. We're discouraged from discussing how much money we have, and we worry about being perceived as greedy for wanting to earn more—or, at least, saying so out loud—especially if we have a job that we love. (The Smart Cookies definitely do *not* subscribe to this belief. It's one of many myths about money we'll discuss in this book that keep women from earning what we're worth.)

You probably have no problem telling your girlfriends about the great deal you got on that Isaac Mizrahi dress at Target. But have you ever compared earnings or investment strategies over cocktails?

Until we formed the Smart Cookies Money Group, we hadn't either. In fact, we would consciously keep from talking about how much money we had, made, or owed, to avoid making anyone uncomfortable, including ourselves. Instead, we'd steer the conversation toward more neutral topics like dating or shopping or the last great book we read. We didn't want to find out that our friends were making a lot more than we were or to admit that our paychecks weren't as big as we wished they were. Some of us were embarrassed to disclose how much credit-card debt we had or, worse, to admit that we had no idea what our bank-account or credit-card balances were.

Whatever the reason we gave, we know now that our collective refusal to discuss our money problems only made them worse, and that our explanations were really all just excuses. Do any of these sound familiar?

IF I DON'T ACKNOWLEDGE MY DEBT, MAYBE IT WILL GO AWAY
(Robyn)

I used to live by the motto "ignorance is bliss" when it came to money: If I didn't think or talk about my growing debt, I thought, I wouldn't have to worry about it. Of course, I knew deep down that it was there. But I figured I'd pay it off at some point. In the meantime, I just didn't want to stress out about it. So I avoided looking at my ATM receipts and credit-card statements. I rarely even kept track of my bank balance (it was usually so depressingly low). I regularly went over my checking-account limit and paid extra fees as a result. But if my debit card was declined, I'd just pull out a credit card. That would explain why, at the time I joined the Smart Cookies Money Group, I had nearly $12,000 in debt.

I'M NO GOOD WITH MONEY, SO WHY TALK ABOUT IT?
(Angela)

I didn't like to discuss money because that would have meant revealing my ignorance on the topic. I remember being so clueless about my finances when we had our first money-group meeting that I actually had to check with my then-boyfriend to find out how much we had in our bank account and what we paid on our mortgage each month. It is awful to admit, but I handed my paychecks over to him every two weeks and he essentially handed me an allowance. At the time it seemed like the right decision. He was good with money, and I thought I wasn't (something I laugh about now). He liked reviewing our finances, and at the time I'd convinced myself that looking at numbers on a spreadsheet was boring. He told me he had everything under control, and I believed him. I rarely spoke up about our finances because I felt I didn't have much credibility. The result? I wasn't even sure where to find any of our financial documents or how much equity in our home I was entitled to claim when we separated.

I DON'T WANT MY COLLEAGUES TO THINK
I CAN'T KEEP UP WITH THEM
(Sandra)

Since my friends and I never talked about how much money we made, I'd assumed that Andrea, with her well-kept hair, Seven jeans, and designer sunglasses, had it all together and wouldn't relate to my financial problems. Andrea and I both worked at the same company, but I never asked how she afforded her elegant attire. That seemed impolite. I just figured that if she could, I should be able to too. I had been really disciplined when I'd lived at home with my parents, automatically depositing a portion of my paycheck into a savings account. I'd put away nearly $8,000. But saving money became a much bigger challenge once I moved out on my own and was suddenly responsible for covering my room and board and everything else. Within months, I went through the money I had saved up and charged another $2,000 on my credit card, going out and trying to keep up with Andrea and my other well-dressed colleagues. I was shocked (and a little relieved) to learn at our first money-group meeting that Andrea had the most debt of all of us: nearly $18,000.

WHAT WOULD MY FRIENDS SAY IF THEY KNEW THE TRUTH?
(Andrea)

I felt a lot of pressure to keep up my professional appearance, and I had told myself that I needed to maintain a certain image to be successful in my career. Of course, there's nothing wrong with looking polished and put together. But for me, that was just an excuse to spend a lot of money I didn't have on pricey designer clothes and too many dinners out with friends that I wanted but knew I couldn't really afford. I may have looked like I was wealthy, but I was anything but. I was in such financial straits at the time we formed our group that I had begun avoiding the phone for fear of facing another call from the credit-card company—or, worse, one from a collection agency. If Sandra had continued trying to keep up with me, she probably would have ended up in the same financial predicament. Of course, until I became a Smart Cookie, I did my best to make sure that no one knew how I'd paid for all those clothes. I was petrified that the people I liked and respected would think I was a failure if they found out how much debt I had accumulated trying to maintain a lifestyle I couldn't afford.

I DON'T WANT TO STOP SHOPPING!
(Katie)

As a public-relations manager, I was making a lot of money for some-one my age, and I figured I deserved a nice wardrobe ("nice" meaning expensive, of course). But I must have known deep down that my spending was a little out of control. I looked forward to my fiancé's golf outings so I could go shopping and stash away new purchases before he came home. I would scurry around trying to hide the evidence, put-ting the cut-off tags and shopping bags at the bottom of the trash bin. When he'd ask whether an outfit I'd bought was new, I'd lie and tell him he'd seen it before. Then one afternoon, after I'd bought a $300 pair of True Religion jeans, I forgot to tuck the receipt away in my wal-let. My fiancé spotted it and asked if I had really spent this much on yet another pair of jeans. I felt my heart race, and my face grew red. He was flabbergasted by this kind of spending—especially since I owned nearly a dozen pairs already. And I couldn't explain the pur-chase to him, or to myself. I knew it was time to get help, or, I feared, my spending habits could cause long-term damage to our relation-ship, not just our bank account. I realized I'd been afraid of talking about money with my friends or with my fiancé, because that meant acknowledging the hundreds of dollars I was spending, or charging, on new clothes each month—and it might mean the end of my shop-ping sprees altogether! By the time we formed the money group, I had about $3,000 in credit-card debt, almost all of it from shopping. That was something I definitely didn't want to admit to my fiancé, my friends, or myself. But I did. (And, by the way, I am as stylish as ever. I just became a smarter shopper. But we'll get to that in Chapter Four.)

In fact, we all confessed the details of our financial situations in that first meeting: how much we made, how much we owed, and how much we needed to learn about managing our money. It was scary and a little embarrassing.

But it was also a great relief. Admitting our own money mistakes, and learning about those that our peers had made along the way, actually made us feel less anxious about our situations and created an immediate bond between us. The real reason none of us had wanted to talk about money was because that would force us to take responsibility for the mistakes we'd made—or were still making. But we quickly realized that it was only once we started talking about the less-than-ideal state of our finances that we were finally able to do something about it.

It was comforting for each of us to know that four other intelligent, successful women—who, by outward appearances, seemed perfectly put together—faced similar financial challenges. We learned that even though our incomes were different, we had each been struggling with similar issues. There was no reason to tackle them on our own. We all had concerns and questions about our finances. Now we also had one another to provide answers, support, and advice; to hold us each accountable; and to keep us motivated as we worked toward our financial goals. That gave each of us a renewed sense of commitment and confidence.

As we mentioned in the introduction, you don't need to be in a money group right now to enjoy the same benefits. But if you want to form a money group, skip ahead to the last chapter for a step-by-step guide on how to do it. Once it is in place, you can go back and use this book as a curriculum for your group meetings. At the end of each chapter we've included five exercises we've done ourselves related to that chapter's issues, along with five questions you can answer yourself or use to help fuel the discussions with your fellow money-group members. These sections can also help set the agendas for your money group; there are enough subjects in each chapter to get you started and to keep the conversation going for several meetings. We've done a lot of research too, so you should be able to find the answers within the chapters to any questions that come up in your meetings. (They certainly did in ours.) But if you get stumped, you can e-mail questions to us directly through our website: www.smart cookies.com or at info@smartcookies.com. And if you need extra work sheets or other tools, you can download them from the website as you go along.

We've specifically organized this book so that it can be used for a money group *or* for an individual. So if you decide to do this on your own, don't worry. You're not really alone. As you read this book, think of yourself as the sixth Smart Cookie, an honorary member of our money group. We're sure that you'll be able to relate to aspects of at least one of our stories—and probably more. And if you want to find others doing this on their own, you can always reach out through the forums and community boards on our website.

Maybe you've got a great job but in a low-paying field, or you're just not making enough money at your company to support the life you want. You want to figure out a way to keep the career you love but earn a bigger paycheck for the work that you do. Robyn has. She remained a social worker but more than doubled her income within 18 months after we started meeting. Or, perhaps, you want to change careers or start your own business but aren't sure how to do it. After we formed our money group, Angela and Katie struck out on their own, and Angela even changed fields entirely—from working behind the scenes at a television production company to selling real estate. We'll tell you how they made those successful transitions.

Maybe you're planning to get married and you're worried about how you're going to pay for the wedding and honeymoon, as Katie was. But as we'll reveal, she and her fiancé came up with a plan so that they were able to save enough money to pay for a lavish wedding at a resort in Mexico *in cash* and still have enough left to begin saving for a new home. You'll see how she did it in the coming chapters. If you're in a committed relationship, you may also relate to the experiences Robyn, Angela, and Katie have had managing money with their spouses or serious boyfriends.

Maybe you'll identify most with Andrea—yes, the one who owed $18,000 to her creditors when we met. She's since been able to pay off the credit line she got through her bank and *all* of her credit-card balances and turn her finances around. Or you may just be starting out, like Sandra, who moved out on her own just a couple of years ago and blew through all her savings in a year. She's now been able to stop overspending and save a substantial amount, enough to start planning the purchase of her first home. You're going to learn how each of us accomplished our goals.

But first we want you to get comfortable talking about money. Believe us: It's inspiring to share your achievements and important to be acknowledged for your accomplishments, but it's also beneficial to share your missteps with others and to get their advice and support. Another advantage of sharing with friends? You can learn from others' mistakes instead of making them yourself.

You don't need to tell everyone the nitty-gritty details of your financial situation, but you can't fix your money problems if you aren't even able to articulate them or to ask other people about the strategies they've used to overcome their financial challenges. Plus, the knowledge and support that comes with being willing to share information about money with your peers is incredibly empowering.

In the near weekly meetings we've had since we formed the group in March of 2006, we've definitely overcome any initial discomfort we had speaking about money. We realized that it's not just okay to talk about money with the people we trust, but it's *essential* if we want to be financially successful. Discussing our finances and our financial goals not only helps to hold us accountable, but the more we talk about our dreams the more tangible they become. Plus, you never know: The people you share your financial goals with might be in a position to help you reach them faster. Maybe they'll decide to share some advice that worked for them or they'll mention a high-paying job position they heard about that might be perfect for you, or they'll gently remind you of your larger goals when you're tempted to splurge on something you really don't need.

So, with all the benefits we can get from talking, why are we so reluctant to discuss money? Women can talk endlessly about almost anything—even sex, thanks in part to the popularity of shows like *Sex and the City* that made it no longer a taboo topic—but when it comes to money matters, the conversation stops.

The fact is, many women are still brought up to believe that investing is better left to men and that talking about how much money we earn—whether it be from our job or a stock sale or a real estate investment—is impolite or, at the least, unladylike. Plus, many of us never got a good grounding in financial basics; it can be embarrassing to admit, even to friends, that we don't know what an index fund or a Roth IRA is or that we feel ill-equipped to invest our money ourselves. It's tough to reveal that months after we bought those designer outfits, we're still paying them off *plus* 18 percent interest. It's even tougher to acknowledge that we can't afford the lifestyle we've created for ourselves. If we divulge the truth, we fear, our friends will think we're a failure or, worse, a fraud. (Here's a reality check: Chances are, your friends already know you can't afford it—they know what you do for a living, and they've seen how often you pull out the credit card.)

Men are often conditioned, from an early age, to make money, and they assume that they will. They're encouraged to learn how to invest, to talk about moneymaking endeavors, and to seek out mentors. But for many women, the thought of investing conjures up images of red-faced male brokers shouting out orders on the floor of the exchange in a language we don't understand, or old men in pinstriped suits swapping stock tips as they smoke cigars and sip bourbon in dark, wood-paneled rooms: a world we're unfamiliar with and a little intimidated by. It's difficult to imagine sitting with our girlfriends over cocktails, trading investment tips. But that's less because we think it's boring than because we worry that we don't know enough about the stock market to make investing interesting or to make any money. (Trust us, once you understand the basics of investing and the potential money to be made in the market, you'll be much more excited to talk about it. But we'll get to that in Chapter Seven.)

Ultimately, in spite of the advances we've made in the workplace, women don't get the same kind of guidance about saving or investing, because we still aren't expected to be the main breadwinners. For all the money single men spend on their entertainment, drinks, and audiovisual gear (nearly $2,000 a year, or 50 percent more than single women, according to the Bureau of Labor Statistics), they tend to tuck more away for the future than women do. In 2006, single women, on average, spent more than they earned, while single men's average incomes exceeded their average expenditures by nearly $3,700. (Of course, women are also still paid less, on average, than men.) If women are "taught" anything about money as we're growing up, it's how to spend it. Where do teenage girls go with their after-school job earnings? The mall. And before they start earning real money, girls can use play money to shop. In 2007, Hasbro introduced a new Monopoly Pink Boutique edition aimed at those eight years or older, which was promoted as being "all about things girls love." Hotels and houses were replaced with—you guessed it—shopping malls, clothing boutiques, and hair salons. Instead of buying a home, players could go on lavish shopping sprees, get instant or text messages, or pay their cellphone bill when it was their turn. Mattel's new Fashion Fever Shopping Boutique Playset lets girls shop for Barbie clothes with a Fashion Fever debit card that automatically resets when it hits zero, so the players can keep spending. "I love shopping. You never run out of money!" exclaims one girl in the commercial. If only.

Is it any wonder that by the time we've graduated from college or moved out on our own, we've become seasoned shoppers? But beyond savings accounts and company investment plans, we're often unsure what to do with our money besides spend it. In most cases, it's not that we want to spend our hard-earned money frivolously; it's that we feel uneducated about how to invest it. So we tend to stick to what we know: shopping and (to a lesser degree) savings accounts. And we leave the investing decisions to someone else—an employer, a financial adviser, or a spouse—or put them off until we're well into our 30s or 40s. So, while our male counterparts are buying homes and investing in mutual funds, we're "investing" in our lifestyle.

The result? By the time we're in our mid-20s or 30s, we've got a closet full of fabulous clothes, drawers filled with beauty products, and a home strewn with stylish furnishings. But we've got a dwindling checking-account balance and little money saved for retirement or even more-immediate needs.

Sarah Jessica Parker's character on *Sex and the City*, Carrie Bradshaw, may be a fictional example, but there are plenty of real women who've spent the money they could have used toward a down payment for a home on shopping trips instead. There's no doubt that many women were nodding sympathetically, or cringing, during the episode in which Carrie learns she has to either buy or vacate the apartment she's renting and realizes that she's got no savings in part because she's bought, or charged, an estimated $40,000 worth of shoes. "I will literally be the old woman who lived in her shoes," she laments, after a bank turns her down for a loan, saying she is not a "desirable candidate." (Of course, this being television, a wealthy, divorced friend "lends" Carrie the expensive engagement ring she kept from her failed marriage, so Carrie can afford the down payment. We're never told what transpires afterward, but Carrie remains in her apartment in later episodes.)

There are other important lessons to be learned from that episode as well. When Carrie tells her friends that she received a check from her wealthy on-again-off-again boyfriend/benefactor "Mr. Big" to help cover the down payment, Miranda and Samantha immediately disagree over whether she should accept it. (Fortunately, in the end, as we mentioned above, she doesn't.) As they argue over the merits of accepting a bailout from a man she's not even dating anymore, Carrie's friend Charlotte says the conversation is making her uncomfortable. Why? "Because we shouldn't be talking about money!" To which Miranda responds: "Why not? We talk about everything else." Exactly! We couldn't put it better ourselves. (And that's a perfect retort if your friends put up the same protests as Charlotte did.) Just as important: In the end, it was Carrie's friends—not her ex—who hold her accountable for her irresponsible spending habits and also help her get back on her Manolo-clad feet.

Our taste might not be as expensive, or as excessive, as Carrie's, but many of us share her concern that we won't be able to afford the down payment on the home we want or that we'll be caught short of money when we really need it. We may not talk about it, but that doesn't mean we don't feel it.

Maybe you're afraid that you'll never be able to pay off your debt. Maybe you're nervous that your bad credit will keep you from being able to buy a house. Or that you'll put an unfair financial burden on a boyfriend or spouse. Or that your parents will find out how badly you've managed your money on your own and be disappointed in you. Whatever your concerns are, trust us, you are not alone. But as we've learned, facing your financial fears is the first step in overcoming them.

As we shared earlier, Andrea harbored fears that she'd be paying off her five-figure debt for years and that if others knew what a messy financial state she was in, they'd think she was a failure. She'd worked so hard to create a polished and professional image and was so successful in other areas of her life that she'd even worried about how the rest of us—who were both friends and coworkers—would react when she admitted how much debt she had. (It turns out that while we were surprised, we were also incredibly supportive.) Sandra worried that she'd have to ask her parents for help or move back in with them. Katie was afraid that her money problems would put a serious strain on her upcoming marriage. Angela and Robyn had just emerged from relationships in which they'd either given up all financial control to their partners or mismanaged their joint funds, so they were both scared about having to handle their money on their own.

But within a few months all of these fears had vanished. We admired Andrea for taking responsibility for her debt and committing herself to getting rid of it. Sandra was able to rein in her spending so she never had to move back home or rely on a parental loan to pay off her debt. Katie's marriage is stronger than ever. And the remaining two of us realized that our financial state wasn't a permanent condition, that we were perfectly capable of improving it on our own—especially with the support of the other Smart Cookies. We all found that just talking about our concerns truly helped ease the burden of carrying them.

For your first exercise, we want you to write down your financial fears. We suggest you use a notebook. You'll be able to keep track of your progress, goals, and improving financial state and use it to complete all the chapter exercises. As you read through this book, we're confident that your fears will start to vanish as well. The fact is: We all have areas we can improve on when it comes to our finances. And we all have the power to make those improvements. We just need the right tools to do it.

With the help of the rest of us, Sandra was able to create a spending plan so she could put away her credit card and stop worrying that her debt would grow so large she'd have to turn to her parents for help. By acknowledging her shopaholic tendencies, Katie was finally able to overcome them. Now she could call the other Smart Cookies for help when she felt tempted to splurge. We also encouraged her to be candid with her fiancé about her past purchases and her intention to curb her spending. Their talk eased her fears that money would be an issue in their relationship and reassured her fiancé that they were working toward the same financial goals. Once Katie became accountable for each item she bought and aware of the more important goals she could be putting her money toward, she was less inclined to purchase another pair of expensive jeans. Not only did their talk ease the tensions that had arisen over their finances but, by enlisting her fiancé's help, she made him part of the solution.

For Andrea, just admitting her debt to her friends and knowing that we wouldn't judge her harshly made her feel a lot better about her financial situation—and about us. And once she learned how to negotiate her interest rates down and then to use her home equity to pay off her credit-card debt entirely, she felt even better. (She'll explain specifically how she did it in Chapter Five.) And Robyn and Angela were able to get, and stay, on top of their finances with the help of the other Smart Cookies.

Knowing we were going to report back every week kept each of us motivated to keep track of how much money we were making and spending. Not only did the other Smart Cookies hold each of us accountable, but we provided tremendous support and encouragement to one another on our journeys to financial independence.

Who would *you* trust with the details of your financial situation? Whose advice or support would you welcome? Who would help you achieve your financial goals and encourage you to pursue your dreams?

In your notebook, list three people who come to mind. They could include your sister, your mother, your best friend, or your spouse. Maybe you feel most comfortable confiding in your favorite aunt or a close friend at work. Think hard about whom you're putting on the list. These should be people you admire and trust. They may end up being other members of your money group. Or, if you decide to do this on your own, they can be mentors, supporters, and resources for you.

Sometime over the next few weeks, whether you do it over the phone or over a bottle of inexpensive wine (which is our preference), ask each of them if they'll share their biggest money mistake with you along with any advice they'd give their younger self. And be ready and willing to share your financial failures too. Don't worry. Your friends have probably made as many embarrassing mistakes as you have, and the ones who seem to have it all together on the outside—with the manicured nails, fabulous wardrobe, and perfectly coiffed hair—are likely the ones hiding the most debt. You may be surprised at how willing they'll be to offer advice and how much better you'll feel after you confess your own mistakes and hear theirs.

P.S.: Hold on to these names: You'll be going back to them in future chapters.

MONEY & MEN

We wrote this book with women in mind, but that doesn't mean men shouldn't be a part of the conversation. While we encourage you to talk with other women about money, it's vitally important to discuss your financial challenges, values, and goals with your partner. It's also fine to turn to him for support, advice, and encouragement.

But a money group provides a different service: The friends and confidantes with whom you choose to share the details of your financial challenges and goals should have your best interest at heart but no real personal stake in your finances (beyond the happiness it will bring them to see you achieve success). Your money-group members are there to provide encouragement, support, and feedback in a confidential setting. Unlike your spouse or partner, they aren't depending on you to pay half the mortgage or to contribute financially toward your mutual goals, so they should be able to focus on what's best for you without worrying about how it might affect them. But it's also important to be candid with your partner or spouse about your intentions for the money group. If you're going to be sharing information about your joint finances, make sure your partner is comfortable with that. Katie had a long talk with her then-fiancé (now husband) before she joined the money group. Not only did he encourage her to join, but he has become one of our biggest supporters. While Katie has improved her own finances and spending habits, the couple has also been able to apply the lessons she's learned to the money they manage together as well. Both of them have benefited from her participation in the group because Katie shares a lot of the information she learns with him. They talk frankly and often about their finances and their financial goals, and they've already achieved many of them—from paying for their wedding in cash to paying off their car loan to saving a significant amount to put toward a new home.

As two of us have learned from personal experience, it can be dangerous to make assumptions about your partner's finances or his financial expectations and habits without finding out the facts. And it can be damaging to your relationship, and to your bank balance, to keep quiet about how your joint funds are saved, spent, and invested and to cede all the financial responsibilities to your partner or spouse. It's true that in most relationships, each person naturally gravitates toward certain roles and responsibilities. It's common for one person in a partnership to feel more comfortable overseeing the day-to-day management of the couple's shared expenses, for example (and don't be surprised if it's you—especially after you've read this book!). It is perfectly fine to designate one of you as the financial caretaker, *as long as both of you agree on it.* Still, regardless of how you decide to split the responsibility for managing your money, the other person should always be in the know, aware of where the money is being spent and invested and how much is in the joint account. Not knowing how your money is being managed can lead to embarrassing and costly situations, as both Robyn and Angela can attest.

Robyn and her then-boyfriend kept their finances separate when they first moved in together; each paid half the rent and joint expenses like utilities and covered their own loans or other payments. But when they got married, they decided to merge their finances. They thought it would be a seamless transition. Boy, were they wrong. Robyn came from more of a working-class family, while her husband's family was well off. But neither of them had received much instruction in how to create a spending plan or manage money. The couple never talked about how their experiences shaped their views on money or influenced their spending habits, nor did they talk about their financial goals or how they planned to manage their money together. They just put all their earnings into one account. Robyn's in-laws also helped them out financially, which was very generous, but their gift didn't come with any guidance. Since Robyn and her husband weren't paying much attention to their finances, having the extra money just gave them an inflated sense of what they could afford. Although they were pretty good about paying their bills on time each month, they often used the leftover money to finance their increasingly indulgent lifestyle. They went on expensive vacations to exotic places, upgraded their cars instead of keeping the perfectly running models they already had, and spent any remaining money instead of investing it or using it to pay down the balances they owed on their credit cards.

There were times Robyn says she worried about their financial situation and tried to talk about changing their approach. But money had become such an issue for them by then, since they'd both racked up considerable debt, that whenever she broached the topic, the conversation often ended with her crying out of frustration or guilt. Robyn earned less than her husband did, so she says she felt more guilt about their predicament and less entitled to speak up about their financial decisions—something she regrets now. Since she and her husband were pooling their funds, they should have each had a say in how the money was used. But part of their problem was that *neither* of them talked about how they should manage their money, nor did they admit that they had little idea how to do it or seek advice from their family or an outside adviser. They hadn't talked about their long-term financial goals, so it's not surprising that they didn't discuss a strategy for saving or investing their money either. They just spent it. By the time their marriage ended, each of them was very good at getting into debt but no better at managing their money.

Angela had similar issues when she and her boyfriend moved in together. But in her case, she ceded most of the control over their joint finances to her partner. We'll let her share her story:

My boyfriend brought home four times more money than I did each month, so I felt like he was entitled to make the major decisions as to where the money would be spent for us as a couple. But then I felt resentment about being left out of the plans and got angry when there was no money left over for what I thought was important (like flying home to see my family or going out for dinners and day trips with my girlfriends). Eventually we stopped striving for shared goals and started planning independent goals but paying for these things from the same pool of money.

If a bill came in—even if it was addressed to me!—it went straight on his desk. I figured it was one less thing for me to stress about, and he seemed to like managing our money. I think by taking care of the finances he thought he was taking care of me and that made him feel good. The more time passed, however, the less I asked about our financial picture and the more in the dark I became. In retrospect, that was a huge mistake. I've now realized it's not about being "good" with math or numbers, it's about taking control of your future and protecting yourself. As I mentioned earlier, when we separated, I didn't know what I had contributed to the relationship or where to even find the related documents.

Not once in our four-year relationship, even during the most intimate of conversations, did we ever delve into our feelings about money.

He assumed I was out of control and spent money carelessly and didn't care about our future, and I assumed that he was too conservative with his money and didn't enjoy what he had worked so hard to earn. These misperceptions probably contributed to our breakup. I have since had many conversations with my ex, who is still a good friend, about the role money has played in our lives. I always thought that his refusal to spend money on trips, dinners, and other purchases for us and for our home was a statement about the way he felt about me and us. I learned that he'd actually thought he was doing what was best for us and our future security: putting more in the bank. He also admitted to me after we broke up that it was stressful at times to have all the financial responsibility on his shoulders. I'd never even thought to ask if he liked doing everything himself. I just assumed he did. And he never thought to ask if I was bothered by not lending a hand in the day-to-day financial matters; he just assumed I didn't care much for it. When it comes to money, never make assumptions. Talk about it!

In the future, I plan to set goals together with my partner and then work as a team to achieve them. And I plan to ensure we talk often and openly about money and to make sure we each play a role in how it's spent, saved, and invested.

We are not focusing on couples in this book, but we do advise that, whether you're already married or you're single and plan to enter into a relationship at some point in the future, you should be totally open about your finances with your partner. You need to recognize and appreciate that you may have different relationships with money and different views on how it should be spent, saved, or invested—and that's okay! What's important is that you both share similar financial goals and are willing to respect and to consider each other's ideas on how to reach them. There is no one right way to manage finances as a couple. We strongly believe that every couple has to find an arrangement that works for each partner.

HOW WE DID IT
(Katie)

As any of the Smart Cookies will tell you, my husband, Nick, and I were complete opposites in our approach to money. I would shop all day long if I could, while he hates to spend money on anything new. Still, we have now developed a financial system that works for us.

Since we began living together, Nick and I brought in a combined income of just under $150,000 in 2007. We're fortunate to earn above-average salaries for people our age. But, though we may earn more than many of our friends, our incomes mattered less when we were coming up with a way to manage our money than did our individual spending and saving styles and our financial goals. Our eventual arrangement evolved to fit our specific incomes and needs, but, with a few adjustments, it could work for any income level. It certainly took a few adjustments on our part before we established a setup that really worked for us.

At first, we decided to split the down payment on our new condominium as well as our monthly mortgage and other bills in half and to contribute evenly toward our other expenses, like groceries, dinners out, and purchases for our new home. We figured we'd just generally try to pitch in the same amount. But while this seemed fair in theory, it didn't work in reality, because we didn't have a system in place for tracking all of our day-to-day expenses. I quickly became frustrated since I always seemed to end up paying for more of the basic household items we needed. It wasn't Nick's fault. But because I did all the cooking and much of the grocery shopping, I estimated that I was spending at least an extra $300 a month on groceries and miscellaneous items like toilet paper and shampoo. I also took on the task of decorating our new home, since I had more of an interest in it, and ended up buying everything from lamps to headboards and artwork. I'm sure Nick would have paid me back half of what I spent, but I often just let it go. Not surprisingly, while Nick's savings grew, my account balance never seemed to top the $1,000 mark. At first I told myself that he was always going to be "the saver" and I would just spend what I made, as I'd done before. These were our roles. But after I joined the Smart Cookies, I decided to take a closer look at how we managed our money. I'm glad I did. We ended up making some minor adjustments to our arrangement, and that led to some major improvements in our savings.

Now Nick and I take out $800 in cash at the beginning of the month from his checking account. We use this amount to cover day-to-day spending like dinners out, drinks, and birthday gifts. The rest of Nick's monthly income covers all of our fixed expenses, including the mortgage, bills, and other items in our spending plan, as well as stock-market investments that we research and decide on together. Since my husband is part of a profit-sharing program at his job, he can earn a little extra some months. We use that for additional investments or we put it into a fund we're using to pay down our mortgage.

Meanwhile, we agreed that all of my salary, except for the $400 I contribute to retirement each month, should go into our joint high-interest savings account. It works in part because the natural "saver" (Nick) is in charge of covering our expenses, while the "spender" (me) is in charge of savings. Knowing that I would have to take money out of a joint account we are using to reach our financial goals makes me much less tempted to spend my salary on impulse purchases or other extras. Plus, we've agreed to allocate $250 a month in our spending plan for me to spend on new clothes—plenty of money to update my wardrobe—which also comes out of Nick's account. On average, we now save around $3,500 a month (my monthly salary minus my retirement contribution). And, if you include the amount we set aside to pay for our

2006 wedding, we saved over $50,000 in just a year and a half! Yes, we're fortunate to both earn good salaries. But even if your incomes are lower than ours, it's possible to save a lot more money than you'd think just by sticking to a specific spending and savings plan that meets your shared financial goals.

Every couple has to figure out what works for them. What I like best about our system is that (1) it has proven that we can live off one person's salary and (2) being in charge of our savings holds me accountable and encourages me to spend less, because not saving not only affects my future now but it also affects my husband's.

smart ⬤ bite

COUPLES & CREDIT: No matter how you decide to divvy up the financial responsibilities with your partner, you may want to keep at least one bank account and debit/credit card in your own name. This is not only important in establishing credit in your name, but it allows you to have some money for personal expenses and for investments that your partner may not want to make with your joint funds. Robyn had no credit in her own name when she was married. And though she and her husband had a joint line of credit of $80,000 when they were together, she was unable to get more than $500 in her name alone after they split up (even though she had almost $120,000 invested into her home!). And remember, regardless of who handles the money, you should be interested and involved in both your personal and your joint finances to ensure that both your credit and your financial future are looking good.

Talk to your husband or partner about your finances. But don't be afraid to talk to your girlfriends about money as well. If we continue to behave as if talking about how we make or manage our money is impolite and unfeminine, we're not taking advantage of one of the greatest, most powerful resources out there for gaining control of our finances: other women! We count on our female friends and family members for help in making other important decisions, from the men we date or marry to the vacations we take to the car we buy. Why not seek their advice and support in figuring out how to earn more money or purchase a place of our own? Instead of bragging to friends about that discounted designer dress, imagine boasting of the 18 percent return you got on your stock portfolio last quarter or the 15 percent raise you negotiated with your boss. Now, that is something to be proud of.

Of course, being candid about money also means facing up to your financial reality—not what you *think* it should be, but what it is today. It's a critical step you need to take to improve your financial situation. No one else can do that for you. In the next chapter, we'll help you figure out your financial weaknesses and strengths and add up all the numbers so you've got a realistic picture of where you are now and what you need to do to reach your goals.

Smart Cookie Summary

Discussion Questions:

You can ask yourself these questions and respond in your notebook. Or, if you're in a money group, use these to get the conversation started at your meetings.

1. Have you ever talked about your finances with anyone else? If no, why not? If yes, who? And how did the conversation go?
2. What do you feel is your biggest financial weakness?

3. What would you most like to change about your current financial situation?
4. What financial advice do you wish you'd gotten earlier?
5. What do you hope to gain by reading this book and/or forming a money group?

Smart Steps:

1. Write down at least one fear you have about your finances.
2. Write down at least one mistake you've made with money.
3. List three or more trusted friends and/or family members whom you would want to belong to your money group.
4. Ask each of them (in person or by phone) if they'll share their biggest money mistake with you, along with any advice they'd give their younger self.
5. Be ready and willing to share your financial foul-ups too!

chapter 2

Know Your Numbers

Four Facts You Need to Know
about Your Finances

Quick, without peeking at your pay stub: Do you know how much you earn each pay period? How much of your check goes into your 401(k) or other retirement account? How much toward taxes?

Do you know how much you owe right now on your credit cards? Your school loan? Your car loan? Your mortgage? Or how much interest you're paying each month on your debt?

If you're like most people, you probably don't know the answers to any of these questions offhand. And it might take hours—or days—to dig up all the documents to get the information. In a random sample of female subscribers to our website, fewer than 30 percent knew offhand how much money they earned last year in net (after-tax) income from their job.

Take a moment to find your most recent paycheck. Now write down how much you're making each month. Do you think it's enough to cover all your current expenses and still allow you to set aside money toward bigger goals like going back to school, buying a new home, or just paying off your debt so your creditors will get off your back?

By the end of this chapter, you'll know the answer—and it may surprise you!

THE REALITY CHECK

For this exercise, you'll want to gather all your pay stubs, bank and loan statements, and utility, cell phone, and credit-card bills from the last three months (or as far back as you can within that period). If you use online banking, this shouldn't take long at all. If you don't, now would be a great time to set up access to your accounts online. You should also get a record of your debit-card purchases and any receipts you have for cash purchases. These documents will help you put together an accurate portrait of how much money is coming in and going out, and where it's going. Use the statements and pay stubs to complete these four statements in your notebook:

> FACT 1: Each month, I make _____ (gross)
>   and_____ (net).

Your gross income is what you make on average before taxes, while your average net income is what you actually take home each month after taxes are deducted. If you typically receive commissions, bonuses, or contract work as well, take the average of what you earned over the three-month period.

> FACT 2: Each month, I owe _____.

This is the combined total of the minimum payments you owe each month to your landlord and your creditors. This includes payments on credit-card debt, school or car loans, or a mortgage.

> FACT 3: Each month, I save _____ and invest _____.

This is the amount you put in a savings account, and the amount you contribute to a Roth or retirement account, or an investment fund, as well as any money you invest in CDs, stocks, or bonds.

FACT 4: Each month, I spend _____.

This is roughly the amount you spend on everything else each month—from the average amount you pay per month for utility bills to haircuts to groceries, gym memberships, and eating out. Use your debit purchases and any receipts you have from the last three months to come up with a monthly average. Initially this figure will be more of an estimate than a calculation. You can compare the first number you come up with to the actual tally you add up once you start keeping track of your daily purchases. (We'll get to that later in this chapter.)

We recommend you make three or four photocopies of the work sheet on on pages 28 to 31 to help you as you add up your numbers. Or you can download copies from our website (www.smartcookies.com). If you're married or in a serious relationship and you're managing your finances together, you can fill out the work sheet together as well. Or, if you prefer, you can each do the exercise separately, based on your individual earnings and expenses, and then compare notes.

You may be surprised by what you learn as you go through your statements. We were.

COFFEE CAN BE COSTLY
(Andrea)

I was aware of how much I had to pay each month on my mortgage, maintenance, utilities, and other bills. But I had no clue how much I was spending on miscellaneous stuff. When I added up my numbers, I was shocked to discover that I was spending, or charging, an additional $1,500 a month outside of my groceries and bills, on things like coffee, clothes, and dinners out—way more than I had imagined. I was spending more than $100 a month on coffee alone! That definitely helped explain all the debt I was carrying and made me much more

SPENDING SNAPSHOT—NEED-TO-KNOW NUMBERS

	Month 1	Month 2	Month 3	Monthly Average (Monthly Totals/3)
MONEY I MAKE				
Wages				
Extra Earnings				
Income Totals				
MONEY I SPEND				
Utility Bills				
Maintenance				
Cable/Internet				
Cellular Telephone				
Home Telephone				

Water Bill			
Home Repairs/Decor			
Groceries			
Meals Out			
Gas			
Car Insurance			
Public Transportation			
Parking			
Gym Membership			
Health Insurance			
Life Insurance			
Home Insurance			

MONEY I SPEND (continued)

	Month 1	Month 2	Month 3	Monthly Average (Monthly Totals/3)
Clothing				
Entertainment				
Other				
Other				
Other				
MONEY I SPEND TOTALS				
MONEY I SAVE				
Investments				
Savings Account				
MONEY I SAVE TOTALS				

MONEY I OWE	Month 1	Month 2	Month 3	Monthly Average (Monthly Totals/3)
Credit Cards (or Credit Line)				
Car Loan				
Student Loans				
Mortgage/Rent				
MONEY I OWE TOTALS				
Total Earnings				
TOTAL EXPENSES				
Cash Short/Extra				

conscious of every purchase I made after that. I also realized that if I could just cut back on my spending for unnecessary stuff, I could pocket $500 to $750 a month after I paid all my bills. That gave me more incentive to pay attention to how I was spending my money.

IT'S NOT JUST ABOUT SPENDING LESS
(Robyn)

Until the first Smart Cookies meeting, I had no idea how much money was coming in each month. I just knew that I was consistently spending more than I was making, even though I was hardly living extravagantly. When I looked at my records, it sunk in just how little I was making. There were definitely places where I could cut back my spending, but I realized that I also wanted to earn more money—a challenge as a social worker. I wound up going back to school to get my master's degree and doubling my income. If I hadn't faced the fact that I was unhappy with what I was making, I'm not sure I would have taken those steps so soon to boost my salary.

LITTLE SHOPPING TRIPS ADD UP TO BIG BILLS
(Katie)

I knew what my salary was when I got my public-relations job, but my actual paycheck fluctuated each month depending on the bonuses and commission I made. So I never really kept track of how much I was actually bringing in each month. I'd never taken the time to add the numbers up or look at where exactly that money was going. I just knew that if I had anything left over between pay periods it meant more money for shopping! And when I ran out of cash before my next check arrived, I pulled out a credit card. I rarely dropped a lot of money at one time, but my shopping trips added up. I was astonished to find out how much credit-card debt I'd accumulated despite making a good salary. It was a serious reality check for me. I realized I couldn't keep spending like that, especially since I was getting married and my spending habits would no longer just affect me.

ESTIMATES AREN'T GOOD ENOUGH
(Sandra)

I had actually taken the time to put together a spending plan before we formed our money group, filling in the blanks with estimates. But then I never plugged in what I actually spent. Once I did, I had a much better idea of how I'd racked up $2,000 in credit-card debt. I had a $400 budget in place for my miscellaneous spending. But I discovered that I was actually spending more than $800 each month! Most of the money was going toward new clothes or drinks and dinners out. That would explain the mysterious increase in my Visa bill. To make matters worse, when I looked over my statements I realized I was being charged an interest rate of 19.5 percent on my balance. I was carrying a balance of about $2,000 and I was paying $40 a month—or nearly $500 a year—in interest alone.

LIKING A JOB ISN'T ENOUGH REASON TO KEEP IT
(Angela)

After reviewing my paychecks, it dawned on me that, though I was making $600 a week, I was working so many hours—up to 14 hours some days—that my pay per hour was barely minimum wage! I really loved working at the TV production company, but when I looked at my finances, I realized I could never afford the life I wanted if I stayed in my job. I had all of these goals I wanted to accomplish in my life but no plan, and no money, to get there. The realization helped push me to make a major career change and go into business for myself, a decision that has really paid off.

(We'll share more details on how Angela did it in Chapter Six.)

Where Does the Money Go?

Did you fill in all of the blanks in the exercise above? Great. Now that you have calculated how much you earn, owe, save, and spend, it's time to take a harder look at where most of your money is going. Over the next few weeks, we want you to keep a daily log of your spending. You should include every purchase you make outside of your monthly bills, mortgage, or rent, and any loan or credit-card payments. You can use the same notebook you've used to do the other exercises and keep it with you. If you forget to bring it, just save your receipts and then write down your totals at the end of the day. After just a few days of keeping track, you should be able to get an idea of your typical weekday or weekend expenses, though we recommend that you continue writing down what you spend for at least a month. It's easier than you think to keep track of your spending, especially once you get into the habit. And now you'll have an answer to that nagging question that pops up when you go to the ATM and marvel at how low your account balance is: Where did all my money go?

To help you figure out the reasons behind your spending patterns, it's also helpful to keep a spending diary, in which you can jot down your thoughts before and after you spend money or use your credit card. When you have time, take a moment before you make a purchase to write down how you're feeling. If you run out for a coffee every weekday afternoon, for example, write down how you're feeling just before you head out. Ask yourself: What would happen if I skipped the coffee today? Or just went for a walk instead? Or if you find yourself wandering into a store where you know you'll

smart **SC** bite

SURPRISE SAVINGS: Looking over your financial documents may also reveal immediate, painless ways to start saving more money. When Robyn examined her bank statements, for example, she realized she was paying as much as $50 a month on bank fees, mostly for having too many debit-card withdrawals. She cut those back to avoid the charges and was able to save $600 in one year. Andrea had also been paying fees for too many debit transactions without even realizing it. When she examined her statements, she learned her bank was treating her online bill payments like transactions, often pushing her over her monthly limit. Andrea immediately did some research and switched her account to a bank that allowed her to make as many transactions per month as she wanted to for free. By doing so, she saved more than $360 a year in fees.

be tempted to make an impulse purchase, ask yourself: Why am I here? What triggered my decision to come here? How do I feel? Is this something I really need? If I thought about it overnight, would I come back? This exercise will also give you a little time to think about the purchase you're about to make. It may even keep you from buying an item impulsively or for the wrong reasons: because you're bored or unhappy, for example, or just because it's a habit.

You can also write down in your notebook how you feel after you make a purchase. Each time you buy something nonessential, ask yourself: On a scale of 1 to 10, how happy am I with the purchase I just made? Do this often enough and you might see some areas right away where you can trim your expenses and find ways to redirect your spending so that it brings you more satisfaction.

By keeping track of purchases, you'll also get a much better idea of how much buying you've been doing unconsciously and you'll become much more attentive to how you are spending your money now. We found that the aware-ness alone was often enough to keep us from making an unnecessary pur-chase. Why? One big reason so many of us get into trouble is that we spend mindlessly. We often don't stop to think about whether we're getting actual enjoyment out of the purchases we make or whether there's a cheaper alter-native that would make us just as happy. Ever buy a shirt because the sales-person convinced you that you looked great in it, only to have it hang in your closet for months? Or come home from the grocery store with impulse pur-chases you barely remember putting in your cart? Or order an appetizer because the waiter recommended it, even though you weren't that hungry? We often spend money for someone else's benefit and not our own—the salesperson who wants to earn commission, the waiter who recommends the expensive bottle of wine to get a bigger tip, the retailer who places items by the register precisely so shoppers will pick them up as they wait in line. So much of what we spend money on gives us very little return on our invest-ment.

If you're skeptical, try this exercise. Close your eyes and imagine what you would grab if your home caught fire and you were told you had five min-utes to gather items you wanted to keep. (We're assuming that any people or pets you live with have already safely escaped.) What would you save? The $150 pair of designer jeans in your closet? The Bose speakers you bought for your iPod? The $60 bottle of perfume you splurged on during a recent trip to the mall? Probably not.

Our guess is that you're more likely to reach for the photo albums filled with irreplaceable images of your friends and family, or the high school year-book signed by your classmates. Maybe you'll try to salvage the bracelet your parents gave you when you graduated from college, or reach for a sweater your grandmother knitted for you or the first drawing you (or your child) made.

When we asked ourselves that question, almost all of us mentioned photos of friends, family, and memories that we cherished. One of us shared that she still had a worn-out blanket from her childhood that had enormous sentimental value. Another mentioned her journal because it was the only, or the best, record of some of the memories and thoughts she really treasured.

Of course, if we were to put any of those items up for sale on eBay, we wouldn't get much money for them. But they're priceless to us. If you think of the gifts you've received that have meant the most to you, chances are they'll have more sentimental than monetary value. A price tag isn't always an accurate gauge of how much value an item will have for us.

It's also important to remember that we're often seeking intangible benefits when we spend our money. So once we realize our motives, we can discover ways of getting the same rewards for less money.

If it's quality time that you want with your friend, for example, does it really matter whether it's over a $50 bottle of wine or a $2 cup of coffee? If you want to show your mom how much you care about her, giving her a framed photograph of the two of you for her birthday would probably mean more than buying her another bottle of perfume or a cashmere sweater—even though it costs less. If you want to feel pampered, you don't need to spend $100 on a massage. For a fraction of the cost, you can buy a bottle of bubble bath, a scented candle, and a CD of your favorite music and treat yourself to several relaxing sessions in your tub. If you're depressed, investing in some real therapy instead of "retail therapy" will make you feel a lot better in the long run. Plus, it may even be covered by your health insurance, so it'll cost you a lot less. If it's a cultural experience you're after, see if your employer has a relationship with any of the local museums so you can get a discount. Or check out some of the free events in your area. Cities often sponsor free outdoor movies or concerts in the summer. Bookstores host free readings by famous authors. Art galleries are also free to the public (assuming you don't buy the art). There are a myriad of ways to have amazing experiences yourself and with your friends for just a few dollars, or for no money at all. We'll give you more suggestions in Chapter Four.

As you add up how much you spend with your discretionary money—on movies, mocha lattes, or manicures, for example—you'll also get an idea of what your priorities are. If socializing is really important to you and you don't want to cut back on your nights out, try meeting friends for a drink after work instead of dinner and just sharing a snack at the bar if you're hungry. (The prices on the bar menu are usually lower than those on the restaurant menu, but the items can still be filling.) You can always prepare a sandwich at home before you head out for the night, or pick up a slice of pizza en route home to satisfy any lingering hunger pangs. Maybe monthly wardrobe updates are a priority for you (and we'll help you trim costs there in Chapter Four), but eating out every night is not. Why not save more for clothes by buying groceries and eating in more often? If drinking a cup of coffee is an integral part of your morning routine, consider brewing your own. Want to make your own lattes on the cheap? Invest in a $20 portable coffee press and a $10 battery-powered milk frother. They're not only easy but fun to use. You could also make your coffee at work or just pick it up someplace besides a specialty coffee retailer to save a little extra money. A large latte at Dunkin' Donuts can cost 50 cents less than one from a premium coffee retailer.

As each of us examined our habits, we realized we were all spending a lot more money eating out than we needed—or even wanted—to do. Robyn figured she was spending about $125 a week by eating lunch out and buying two coffees every day. By bringing her lunch to work, cutting back on the caffeinated beverages, and eating dinner at home more often, she was able to save more than $250 each month. For Sandra, going out to concerts and movies took precedence over other expenditures. So she canceled her cable service, which was costing $60 a month, and put that money toward her entertainment budget. She also limited herself to spending $100 a week on entertainment, which she took out in cash and put in an envelope at the beginning of each week so she wouldn't be tempted to overspend.

Once you've kept track of your purchases for a month, go back to the work sheet you photocopied from pages 28 to 31 to fill in the blanks. Again, you can also download it from our website at www.smartcookies.com. This time, the figures you fill in should be much more accurate. They will help you see exactly where your money is going in an average month. And you'll also see how different your actual spending is from your estimates.

In the next chapter, we're going to help you create a revised spending plan for the upcoming months so that you can be confident your money is going where it will give you the most joy and bring you closer to reaching your goals.

Keeping track of where your money goes should help you discern your spending patterns, but it's also important to understand *why* you make the decisions you do.

How often have you made an impulse purchase and regretted it later? Maybe you were stuck in line waiting to check out and ended up buying a gossip magazine and a bag of chocolates (not particularly good for your mental, physical, or financial health!). Or you went shopping for a dress and ended up picking up some cute earrings too, just because they were featured on sale near the register. How often have you spent more than you intended on an outfit for a particular occasion because you didn't have the time or the energy to shop around?

COOKIE CONFESSIONS
(Sandra)

I am definitely guilty of splurging for a "special" occasion. I once paid more for my outfit than my date spent to take me out! When he asked me to go to an exclusive, expensive downtown restaurant, I was worried that I didn't own anything dressy enough to wear. (Of course, I realized later that this was just an excuse to go shopping.) I spent the entire day combing the city for a new dress. Initially, I tried to be sensible. I started out scouring the racks of stores offering discounts or sales, but nothing seemed to fit quite right. The last stop on my search was a Betsey Johnson boutique. I tried on three dresses, and the last one seemed perfect—until I looked at the price tag. It was $500! But I had only an hour left before I was getting picked up. At this point, I'd worked myself into a serious panic, and I was sure I wouldn't have time to find something else. So I bought the dress. Needless to say, the guilt of spending so much on a dress I knew I might wear only a few times lasted a lot longer than the relationship.

Of course, Sandra is hardly the only one who's overspent preparing for a date. We all found that dates were a great excuse for spending too much on new clothes and trips to the salon—even if we weren't that into the guy who'd asked us out and only ended up going out with him once or twice. Looking our best meant buying new clothes and paying for manicures and haircuts—and even expensive accessories for our pets. Robyn once boasted to us that she'd managed to set up the least costly date yet: a coffee and walk with her dog and her date through the park. Then the next time we met, she admitted sheepishly that, just before the date, she'd splurged on a $150 designer dog collar and leash! To her credit, she agreed to cut the $100 she set aside each week for "fun" spending by $50 the next week to compensate. (We'll discuss the "fun" money concept more in Chapter Four.) We know there will be slipups like Robyn's. Each of us went over our spending limits sometimes. But a good way to respond is to acknowledge you overspent and then compensate by cutting costs the next week.

Now we're a bit savvier about how much we spend before a date too. Instead of buying a new outfit, we raid one another's closets. Instead of spending time at a salon, we allow a little more time at home to primp and pamper ourselves. And we've set up a Smart Cookie "hotline" system for those rare occasions when we're tempted to buy a designer dress or dog leash, or another extravagance, before a date. We each have a designated Smart Cookie to call who will remind us of the many ways we'd rather use that money.

Another common culprit: spending money out of a sense of guilt or obligation. Maybe you realize you forgot an old friend's birthday, so you panic and order a fancy bouquet of flowers at the last minute—paying extra for same-day delivery—when, instead, you could have called her and apologized, then sent a gift belatedly that would last a lot longer than flowers and cost you less. Maybe you felt bad because you missed your coworker's last party, so you feel compelled to attend this one *and* bring along a pricey bottle of wine. Maybe you spent more than you wanted to on a baby-shower gift for your wealthy cousin, even though you aren't that close, just because she sent you an expensive sweater for your birthday. Or you pitched in the same amount as everyone else at a work dinner even though you only had a glass of water and a salad, while your colleagues ordered steak, dessert, and a couple of $12 cocktails.

When we added it all up, we found out that we were sometimes spending as much (or more) on dinners or gifts for people we weren't very close to as we spent on our good friends or boyfriends. That's just wrong.

Katie still cringes when she recalls buying a $45 potted orchid plant as a housewarming gift for a colleague she hardly knew. Andrea says she often treated friends to drinks or to dinner if they'd treated her before, even if the bill had been substantially smaller when they did it. She says she always felt like she had to return the favor, even though her friends never gave any indication that they expected to be repaid for their generosity. And if she was the one who suggested meeting for coffee, she often found herself picking up the tab because she worried she'd look cheap otherwise.

Sandra once offered to help set up at a colleague's small wedding, running errands and helping the family decorate. When the mother of the bride realized some items were missing from the buffet, she asked if Sandra would mind running out to "pick up a few things." Sandra ended up buying $70 worth of groceries with her own money! No one offered to reimburse her, and she felt rude asking. But she could think of several ways she would have preferred to spend that money.

Emotional spending is also a persistent problem for most women. Who hasn't "treated" herself to a shopping splurge or a trip to the salon to try and lift her spirits—even if it has the opposite effect on her bank balance?

After Sandra and her longtime boyfriend broke up, she was desperate to get away for a weekend. Early one Saturday morning, on a whim, she began surfing the web for flights to Calgary, where her best friend lived. She found a flight that left a few hours later, charged the tickets to her credit card, packed up, and left. Though she says it was comforting to spend that weekend with her friend, she could have gotten the same support just by picking up the phone. Had she allowed herself even an hour to think the trip over and decide whether or not to buy the ticket, she probably would have changed her mind—and saved herself a $600 charge on her credit-card statement.

That's one good reason why, when it comes to finances, you absolutely have to plan ahead and prioritize. Otherwise, it's easy to spend mindlessly, or emotionally, without thinking about the consequences until it's too late. Reaching your financial goals doesn't require eating ramen noodles for dinner, swearing off shopping, or spending weekend nights on the couch. You don't have to give up one thing, like shopping, to have the other—say, a down payment. But in order to achieve your larger financial goals, you need to make some adjustments in the short term. And, trust us, if you're aware of how much you need to set aside each month for a down payment on a home—and how badly you want that home—you'll be less tempted to overspend next time you're at the mall or the grocery store.

Katie had to ask: Did she really need 12 pairs of jeans? Or was she just shopping to fill a void? Andrea told us she was surprised at how much she was spending on expensive dinners out with friends and colleagues and wondered why she spent so much. Would it matter much if she went out for drinks or brunch instead? Or ordered in? She decided it didn't, and we agreed. And as we mentioned earlier, all of us realized we were sometimes simply spending money out of obligation or peer pressure—attending a friend of a friend's wedding simply because she'd invited us, or agreeing to meet colleagues at an expensive restaurant because we didn't want to feel left out. If we wanted to reach our financial goals, we realized, we had to be a bit more selective about where we put our money and why. (We'll get into how we did this in more detail in the next chapter.)

Of course, we're not alone. In interviews we conducted with a random sample of female subscribers to our site, most of them in their 20s and 30s,

30 percent said that they felt pressured to purchase items and to maintain a certain lifestyle. Nearly six out of ten said they consistently overspent on entertaining and socializing—mostly, dining or drinking with friends and colleagues—and half said they spent too much on clothes and shoes.

If you are regularly overspending, ask yourself: Who are you trying to impress by pretending you can afford more than you can? Is it your boyfriend? Chances are he couldn't care less whether the Prada purse you're carrying is real or not. In fact, if he's like most men, he probably hasn't noticed your purse at all. Your family? They probably know the truth anyway. (They did see your apartment, after all.) Your friends? They love you for the witty, wonderful woman you are—not the labels you wear. (And if they don't, you don't need a new wardrobe, you need new friends!) Yourself? Why try to fool yourself? Avoiding the truth not only keeps you stuck in your situation, but it reinforces the belief that you're powerless over it. And you know that's not true.

While you're examining your spending habits, it's also helpful to look further back than last weekend's shopping spree. Many of your financial views and patterns were likely formed when you were younger by observing how your parents handled their money and through your own experiences with money growing up. This was certainly the case for us.

Katie remembers that the only time she and her father discussed the concept of budgeting was just before she left for college. She asked how much money she'd need to pay for rent and the cost of living in the city, and they went over some approximate amounts. It was only much later, when she was actually out on her own, that she realized how much they had underestimated what city life would cost. But because she had worked through school and landed a good-paying job after graduating and never asked her parents for money, they assumed that she was doing fine financially. She didn't tell them about her shopping habits, but she says now that it's not hard to see where they came from. Shopping trips were an essential part of her childhood, something she associated with happy memories of spending time with her parents and of getting new clothes or dolls that she really wanted (though, of course, she didn't have to pay for them then). Her parents, in trying not to deprive her, inadvertently gave her an excuse to justify the many shopping trips she'd later indulge in on her own. She remembers her dad telling her that they weren't hurting for money, so if she really, really loved something, there was no reason she shouldn't have it. Though she only took advantage of that a few times growing up, she says that once she was on her own she often used that motto to justify her own buying habits. She managed to convince herself that she really, really loved and needed *everything*.

Our grandparents grew up during the Great Depression, so our parents learned firsthand the importance of living within their means and setting aside money in case of emergencies. But these lessons were often lost on our generation because we grew up in a time of greater affluence. Our parents didn't want us to go without if they could help it and, in some cases, *they* were our "emergency fund." Because most of us didn't know how our parents paid for our home, toys, clothes, activities, and other expenses, we simply drew our own conclusions. Often, as we've realized, the assumptions we made turned out to be wrong or, at least, only partly true.

YOU SPEND *YOUR* MONEY, WHY CAN'T I SPEND MINE?
(Andrea)

Both my parents always worked hard (and still do) for their money. But they also liked to enjoy it. Growing up, we regularly went on vacation, lived in a nice home, rode in nice cars, and my parents covered my and my brother's college tuitions. My brother and I were given every opportunity in life because my parents had the financial means to support us and encourage us. I was rarely turned down when I asked for money; my parents were pretty lenient when it came to providing financially for us. My assumption, from observing my parents, was: You work hard, you play hard. I didn't realize how much they saved and invested to afford the life we had or to pay for our college educations.

Even though my mom always told me to save my babysitting money, I never did because I thought, I worked for it and you guys spend *your* money, so why can't I? I didn't have big expenses then, but it didn't occur to me to save any of that money I made. I always knew that my parents would help me out if I was in financial trouble. I never asked how they managed their own money. And I don't recall them ever telling me the details of how they did it. They taught me some basics, but I didn't want to listen to any lessons on how to budget or discuss specific financial issues I might face once I was out of the house. I assumed that I would just figure out how to do all of this stuff on my own. Instead, I ended up massively in debt and unsure of what to do about it.

Like Andrea, you may have had an after-school job, but your parents probably provided you with most of what you needed. They likely thought they were doing you a favor. They wanted you to have a good upbringing and not worry about money, as they may have growing up. But if they didn't explain how they could pay for expenses, and they didn't discuss how you would manage your money once you were on your own—or didn't have an accurate picture of how much it would cost you to live on your own—they may have inadvertently set you up to make assumptions that could put you in serious financial jeopardy.

Angela's mother, who was divorced, raised Angela and her brother by herself for years until she remarried, working long hours as a nurse. Though Angela now realizes how tough it was for her mother financially, her mom took pains to make sure she and her brother never felt deprived growing up. Unfortunately, that often meant relying on a credit card. Once Angela's mom remarried and she and her new husband worked together to create a plan for the entire family to get out of debt, Angela was able to see just how much their former lifestyle had actually cost.

By trying so hard to provide for her kids and to hide her own financial struggles, Angela's mom had inadvertently provided a distorted financial picture to her kids. Before she joined the Smart Cookies, Angela had become accustomed to spending all the money she made (and sometimes more) in order to keep up her lifestyle—just as her mother had done for her when she was young. She was not interested in saving money for her future when she had so much she wanted to do and have in the present. Until she joined the Smart Cookies and had a frank discussion with her mother, she had no idea how much providing everything Angela wanted as a child had cost her mother.

SPEND NOW, WORRY LATER
(Angela)

Growing up, I don't ever remember seeing cash. My mom seemed to charge everything to her credit card. I remember being in a convenience store when I was little and my mom using her credit card to pay for a bag of M&Ms for me. For a long time, I honestly thought that was how you paid for things: with this small piece of plastic. Only years later did I realize that my mom paid for so many of the things she bought for me with her credit card because she did not have any other means.

After my parents' divorce, my mom went back to school to get her nursing degree. When she began her career, she worked with terminally ill patients, and she once had a patient say to her: "Look at me, I have all this money in the bank and I am never going to get to enjoy it. Spend your money along the way, and enjoy it while you can." My mom admits now that she took this advice to the extreme. She spent every single penny and thought that by doing so she was living life to the fullest. I'm sure that's where my former motto of "spend now, worry later" came from. I was spending every cent I had, and no one could tell me otherwise. I always thought, I'd rather have a great trip with my girlfriends and some great memories than a pile of money sitting in a retirement account. Now I realize there has to be a balance.

I think that when my mom was single, she also tried to overcompensate and made an especially nice home for us, filled with all of the things we loved. She didn't want us to miss out on activities that the other kids at school or in the neighborhood were participating in. So we took skiing lessons, wore nice clothes, and even rented homes in some of the area's nicest neighborhoods. My mom grew up in a very poor family, always hearing, "No, we can't afford that." So she worked hard to ensure she would never have to say those words to me or my brother. She really wanted us to have the opportunities that she didn't.

She even went back to school to become a realtor and worked two jobs while my brother and I were growing up. Even then, she wasn't always able to pay for everything, so she used her credit card. My mom has long since paid off her credit-card debt and is in great shape financially today. But we had no idea that by making our lives so easy my mom was making her life that much harder—and by trying to allow us to keep up with our affluent neighbors and classmates, we were actually heading further into debt.

Those of you who, like us, were born in the '70s or '80s were hit with a double whammy: high expectations and declining real income. You probably grew up in relative affluence (even if your parents were going into debt to provide it for you) or, at least, were surrounded by images—whether it was on *Friends* or *Melrose Place*, in movies like *Singles* or *St. Elmo's Fire*, or in the pages of your favorite magazine—of what life was supposed to look like once you were out on your own. When you graduated college or left home and started your first job, you had high expectations. But enjoying a lifestyle similar to the one you had growing up, or the one you envisioned, has become increasingly difficult. Real median income for those under 35 is almost the same as it was in the 1970s (in fact, it's even lower than it was in

1978 for those under 25), according to the U.S. Census Bureau. That means most of you are making the same or less in inflation-adjusted dollars than your parents did at the same age, yet you have more expenses than they did: from cable to computers to cell phones and iPods. Your expectations of how you should live often *can't* be maintained on today's starting salaries. Credit-card companies are well aware of this, and they're only too willing to help cover the difference—plus interest, of course. That only exacerbates the problem. If you aren't planning to work on Wall Street, and your parents don't prepare you for the reality of the cost of living on your own, you can easily have a "successful" career yet barely be able to stay afloat if you aren't proactive about planning ahead. This doesn't mean that you can't take a job that pays less than $40,000 a year and still sock away enough money for a home, a comfortable retirement, and a closet full of stylish clothes. But you have to adjust your short-term spending and your timeline accordingly. That's why it is so important to have a clear understanding of the life that you want, to figure out what you need to get there, and to make a realistic plan as soon as possible.

Chances are that your spending habits now aren't based on a plan but on assumptions: that you will be employed and healthy for a long time, that your salary will increase much faster than your expenditures, and that you'll marry someone who is doing at least as well as (and, hopefully, better than) you are. For now you just try not to spend more than you make and to tuck a few dollars into your savings account, and you may think you're doing pretty well—that is, until your landlord raises the rent or your car breaks down, or your friend gets engaged and asks you to be in the wedding (which, she's decided, will be on a Caribbean island), and you realize you don't have enough cash to cover it. Suddenly you're stuck. So you're forced to drain your savings, or, if your account is already tapped out, pull out that credit card you got in college or the Visa application that just arrived in the mail. Then, months or years later, you're surprised to discover that while you're making a good salary, you don't have the financial security you imagined would come with it. You don't have to be like *Sex and the City's* Carrie Bradshaw to get yourself into debt. It doesn't take much to overspend. If you're not conscious of where your money is going, one big expense could tip you over the edge.

You can't operate on autopilot if you want to be financially successful. You have to be proactive. Otherwise, you could end up veering way off course or, worse, crashing and burning financially. We know that from personal experience.

Each of us was stuck in a downward spiral of short-term spending. Had we continued to behave in the same way without examining our spending habits, we would have been in real financial trouble. That's why it's so important to know your numbers. You have to know what you're making, saving, spending, and charging *now*, so you know how to adjust the figures to achieve your financial goals in the future.

Smart Cookie Summary

Discussion Questions:

1. Where does most of your discretionary money go each month? Why?
2. Can you think of an impulse purchase you made and regretted later, or an occasion when you spent money out of guilt or obligation?
3. What's the most you ever spent preparing for a date?
4. What is your most prized possession? Why?
5. What would you like to be spending more money on? Less money on?

Smart Steps:

1. Gather all your pay stubs, bank and loan statements, and utility, cell phone, and credit-card bills from the last three months (or as far back as you can) as well as a record of your debit-card purchases and any

receipts you have for cash purchases. Add up how much you earn (after taxes), owe, save and invest, and spend each month.

2. Start keeping track of your daily spending and your feelings about those purchases.

3. After you've kept track of your spending for a few weeks, use the work sheet to write down where your money is going (by category).

4. Write down categories where you spent more money than you expected. Think of ways you might trim those costs.

5. Close your eyes and imagine what you would grab if your home caught fire and you were told you had five minutes to gather items you wanted to keep. (We're assuming that anyone or any pets you live with have already safely escaped.) What would you save? For each item, ask: Why is this so valuable to me?

chapter 3

Whose Life Are You Living?

How to Create (& Afford) the Life that *You* Want

Who hasn't gazed at that fabulous little black dress in the store window and imagined herself wearing it? There's a reason why clothing stores spend so much time and money creating the perfect window displays. Retailers know the power of visualization. Yet, when it comes to building wealth and creating the lives we want, we often overlook that powerful tool.

Have you ever stopped to envision what you want your life to look like one year—or five years—from now? Will you still be living in the same apartment or will you be in a new home? Will you be single or married? Will you have kids? Will you have the same job or will you be in a different career altogether?

When we formed the Smart Cookies Money Group, this was one of the first exercises we did. Why? Because we need to remember the reasons *why* we want to make more money and what we're saving all that money for, so it becomes that much easier to do. It's true that a lot of what brings us happiness in our lives can't be bought with money: our friends, our family, and our health. Certainly, money *alone* can't buy happiness. But having money does help you to create the life that you want. Money can't buy you health, but it can buy the best health insurance and medical care available—not to mention the sorts of indulgences that help keep you healthy, like a personal trainer, a gym membership, or a grocery cart full of organic food. Money can't buy you friends (we hope not, anyway). But having money allows you to purchase a home with enough space for entertaining friends on a regular basis, and to share experiences with your friends that you might not otherwise be able to afford, like joining them for an amazing vacation or splurging on dinner at the top-rated restaurant in town. Money can't buy you family, but it can provide the means to visit your relatives regularly wherever they live or to buy a vacation home large enough to host the entire family.

Planning Your Perfect Day

For this exercise, close your eyes and imagine it's a Friday morning a few years from now (we recommend a two- to five-year time frame). Now think about exactly how you'd want to spend the day ahead. And keep in mind that this is a weekday. (We think it's important to consider the kind of work you *want* to be doing—and not just say you wouldn't be working at all on your perfect day.) Use the questions below to help describe your perfect day in your notebook.

1. What time do you wake up, and how are you feeling as you greet the day?
2. Where are you? If you're at home, what does it look like?
3. Who is with you?
4. What kind of work are you doing and with whom? (If you don't know exactly what kind of work you'd be doing, or where, that's okay. But it's important to think about the qualities you want to find in the work you do, and the type of work environment you want.)
5. As you head out to face the day, how do you look? What are you wearing?

6. When and where do you work, and how do you get there?

7. When you're done with work, how will you spend your spare time— and with whom? What activities do you enjoy?

8. What is your evening like? What are you eating and drinking?

9. When you go to bed that night, how are you feeling after spending the day doing exactly what you love?

10. What are you most grateful for and what are you looking forward to as you drift off to sleep?

Allow yourself to imagine all the possibilities. Don't let credit-card debt or a dwindling bank balance keep you from envisioning the future you truly want. This should be a clear snapshot of life exactly as you'd want it to be.

In the space below the description you've written in your notebook, answer these questions:

1. What three activities on your perfect day bring you the most joy?

These could include activities as diverse as: doing work you love, meditating in the morning, and sharing dinner with your family or friends.

2. What are three things in your perfect day that you don't have now?

These could range from a spacious new apartment to a convertible sports car to a baby.

Andrea imagined living in a brownstone apartment in Manhattan, working in a job she loved that allowed her to travel frequently to see her family, and owning a vacation home on Cape Cod. Angela's perfect day included indulging in a relaxing spa massage, sharing strawberry daiquiris with her family on the deck of the beautiful custom-built lakefront vacation cottage she helped purchase, taking a bubble bath, and then curling up with her boyfriend (or husband), a good book, and her favorite candies. Robyn pictured herself remarried with kids, a dog, and a flexible job, living in a dream home that she and her new husband helped design with a gourmet kitchen, oversize living room for entertaining, and a wraparound porch. Katie envisioned herself in a beautiful new home with a baby, cooking in a fabulous kitchen for her family and some of her closest friends.

Whatever you want—no matter how far-fetched it may seem now—should be included in your plan. Write down as many details as you can, so you can truly picture how your life will look. This exercise helped us to see how our current actions did, or didn't, fit into the bigger plans we had for our lives. Having a clear idea of the life we wanted also prompted us to make immediate changes that would help us realize it faster.

Sandra, for example, decided that three things that would bring her joy on a perfect day included owning a loft apartment downtown, working with her friends and having a flexible schedule, and having her evenings free to enjoy good wine and good music with her closest friends and family. After she completed the exercise, she realized that she then had none of the above in her life.

Planning my perfect day helped me realize that there were other things I wanted in my life that were equally important or more important to me than working—even if I had a job I loved. The position I'd found working in public relations at the same company as Andrea and Katie seemed like such a great fit for me that I let it become the focus of my life. That's one reason why the perfect-day exercise was important for me. Before the exercise, I was getting in to work at 6:30 a.m. and working until 5:00 or 5:30 at night and then coming home exhausted. I was often too tired to go out after I left the office. Though I enjoyed my job, I hardly had a life outside it. Now I allow myself time in the morning to do the things I love: going for walks or a run and then going in to work at a sensible time. I also make sure that I take my lunch break. I still save money by preparing my lunch and bringing it in, but I often meet a friend during my lunch hour at the park or call a friend I haven't talked to in a while. ~Sandra

The Power of Positive Thinking

One of the other advantages of envisioning your perfect day is that it reminds you—or should, anyway—that you have a lot of control over your financial destiny. Even if you owe thousands of dollars to your creditors, you have no savings, and you feel like you're on the brink of bankruptcy, it's not too late to turn your situation around. You can still reach your goals, and you can probably do it a lot sooner than you think. Andrea did.

Not only did she have $18,000 in debt when we first met, but one of her credit cards had gone into collections and she was struggling just to cover the minimum payments. She wanted to pay off both of her credit cards and her credit line, increase her salary, and save enough to start working toward her larger goals. Within a year and a half, she had found a new job in marketing and increased her earnings by $20,000 (we'll share more on how she did it in Chapter Six), paid off all of her debt, saved $3,000, and invested an additional $2,000 into her retirement account. That's a huge turnaround!

Now she is well on her way to living her perfect day. But when we first met, she was drowning in so much debt that she had a hard time looking beyond the next billing statement. Maybe it seemed frivolous or pointless to envision living in a brownstone in Manhattan and joining a tennis club when she couldn't even keep up with her credit-card payments. But by allowing herself to envision the life that she wanted, she realized that her current situation was just temporary and she started taking steps immediately to improve it. If you can imagine a positive future for yourself and see your perfect day as attainable (and, believe us, it is), you will be able to stick to your plan for getting there, even in the face of small obstacles like an unexpected car repair or another expense that you hadn't counted on. Just remember to keep your eyes on the prize. Whatever your financial situation is now, it's only a matter of time and persistence until you're able to live your perfect day.

Even as you're thinking about your future, it's also essential to remember the positive things in your life now. Even if your financial situation isn't what you want it to be, we're sure there's a lot you have to be grateful for in your life right now, and it's important to reflect on those things. We don't want you to be so focused on having a better future that you get frustrated with your life today. This is a journey. The habits that we've adopted ourselves and share with you are intended to be lifelong habits. This isn't about finding a quick fix but about developing a new outlook on your finances and your financial prospects and creating new practices and strategies today that can benefit you for the rest of your life. This is about living your best life right at this moment and *every* day. Remember that with each passing hour, you're that much closer to the life of your dreams. Enjoy the ride.

Being grateful for what you have now—whether it's good health, a supportive spouse, a group of great friends, or a home in a city you love—should help you appreciate the goals you'll achieve in the future even more. Taking a few moments each day, week, or month to think about all that other people have done for you should also serve as a reminder of how much you mean to others. Remember, you've got a lot of people rooting for you as you work toward your goals. And don't forget to take a moment to reflect on all that you've already accomplished (even just by picking up this book and reading this far). The fact that you're already taking steps to improve your finances and your life should give you more confidence that you can attain your financial goals, no matter how grand they may seem now, just by continuing in the same direction.

Create a Vision Board

To keep us motivated, we wanted to do more than just imagine and write down descriptions of our perfect days. So we also created "vision boards" that we could look at every day to remind us of what we want to have in our lives and the goals we want to accomplish.

These boards symbolize what is possible if you stick to your plans.

They're meant to serve as motivation, so you can include words, phrases, or images that do just that. You might want to add a picture of someone whose accomplishments inspire you, like Hillary Clinton, Angelina Jolie, or Oprah Winfrey. Your collage can include photos, words, and pictures cut out of magazines, or maybe a postcard depicting a destination you want to visit or a key chain to symbolize the car you want to own—anything that inspires and motivates you.

The day I created my vision board, I instantly had a renewed sense of excitement about the life that I want—and plan—to have. Every morning I take a few minutes before I get out of bed to look at the images and inspirational sayings on the board, which I've hung on a wall in my room, and I close my eyes and imagine myself in the places and with the people pictured on my board. So when I set out each day, I am well aware of the reasons for the choices I make and the purpose behind my actions. I am doing everything in my power to make my vision board a reality, and I know that one day it will be. ~ Angela

What's on Angela's board? Pictures of a lakefront cottage like the one she plans to own, a tranquil beach on Maui's western coast (she's always wanted to visit Hawaii), a couple dancing in the snow (to remind her that she wants a partner who is silly, spontaneous, romantic, and likes to dance), a fit woman with a broad smile jumping on a trampoline (to remind her to work toward her optimum health and to care for her body), a downtown condo she wants to invest in, information on a health spa in Arizona with an itinerary already mapped out, a dollar sign made of pink flowers (for the wealth she wants to attract into her life), and photographs of her with friends and family on various getaways (to remind her to make smart choices so she can have the flexibility and the funds to spend quality time with the people she loves).

Of course, each board is as unique as each of us. Andrea's vision board, for example, includes a photo of a mother with her baby to represent motherhood;

a picture of a Range Rover (her dream car); a house on Cape Cod, where she'd like to vacation every year; a picture of the cabin in Ontario that her family used to own, which she plans to buy back for her family to use again; a picture of a brownstone apartment in Manhattan, where she'd like to live; a woman whose abs she admires running on the beach in a bikini; some inspirational quotes; and a picture of a Cartier love bracelet to symbolize finding her soul mate.

Robyn's vision board has a picture of a beautiful kitchen with a very large table. She has warm memories of sharing dinners with her family and hopes to replicate the experience one day with her own children. The kitchen also represents that beautiful custom-made home she hopes to share with a husband and kids. She has a picture of a cottage overlooking the ocean as well and a photograph of herself traveling through Southeast Asia—an image she likes not just because it depicts her engaging in one of her favorite activities (traveling) but because she had just spent five days a week at the gym for six months and was in the best shape of her life. To inspire her further, she added a picture of a runner to remind her of her goal to participate in a half marathon. Another nonfinancial goal is to train her dog to be better behaved; she's added a picture of a dog sitting obediently. She also has an image of a little girl dancing that she cut out from a card, which symbolizes the sense of independence and free-spiritedness she wants to maintain.

Your vision board can be as simple as a collage of pictures and words you've glued onto a large piece of paper, or you can use a cork bulletin board onto which you've tacked the images you want to include. Whatever form your "board" takes, it should be displayed someplace where you'll see it several times a day: on your desk, on your bedroom or bathroom wall, or inside your closet or pantry. In addition to her actual board, Robyn has two framed photos of places she wants to travel through—India and South America— and one of Venice, a city she loves and has already visited (to remind her that her other travel goals are attainable). To save money, she downloaded photos of each place from the Internet for free and then had them printed, matted,

---

smart **SC** bite

TEST-DRIVE YOUR DREAMS: Want even more incentive? After you cut out photos of your dream car and tape them into your notebook or tack them onto your vision board, spend an afternoon test-driving the car (though we recommend that when you actually buy one, you look for a used model in good condition, which will save you a lot of money without sacrificing style). You can do the same with your dream home. Spend an afternoon with a realtor looking at potential homes and take photos of the one you want and put them in your notebook or on your board, so it seems even more real. If you want to change careers, seek out a mentor who is already doing the job you want. By doing this, you are reinforcing the belief in your mind that you will be living this lifestyle soon. And it's great motivation to adjust your spending habits now so that you can afford that lifestyle sooner rather than later.

---

and framed on her walls. The whole project cost about $30. Not only does it serve as inspiration, but it's affordable and attractive art for her apartment.

Why is it so important to visualize your perfect day and the possessions and activities that really bring you joy? Once you have a clear idea of what truly brings you joy, you'll have a better idea of what doesn't. And you'll be less susceptible to sales pitches or advertisements. Would replacing your perfectly functioning television with a 52-inch plasma screen really make you happy? Or would it just make the salesperson happy? What if you put that $1,200 you saved toward a down payment on a home instead or used it to help pay for the Hawaiian vacation you've always wanted to take?

Advertisers would love you to believe that having an apartment filled with high-end furniture made by their client will bring you joy or that owning a Louis Vuitton bag will make you feel successful, even if you have to pay for the purse with plastic. Or that having a closet full of designer dresses is something to aspire to, even if it's at the expense of saving money for a home—something that might actually *increase* in value. Advertisers care about their client's satisfaction, *not* yours. Salespeople don't care whether you can really afford the product they're pushing on you or whether you have to max out your cards to make that purchase. It's in their best interest to convince you to buy an entirely new living room set instead of just the end table you initially planned to purchase, so that they bring home a bigger commission check. As long as your credit card isn't declined, they're happy to let you use it.

Retailers aren't the only ones who may urge you to make decisions that aren't in your best interest. Unless you are clear in your mind about the career and the salary you want, your boss has every reason to put off promotions and pay you as little as he or she can, to save money. And, if you don't think about the position you want in your company or the ultimate career you hope to have and plan accordingly, your boss is going to put you in a role that serves his or her best interest—but not necessarily yours. You need to know what you want and speak up about it. That's another one of the benefits of planning your perfect day. The exercise should help you think about what you want in *every* aspect of your life, not just your bank account, and inspire you to start taking steps to get there. Even your friends and family may unwittingly push you into making decisions that lead you away from what you truly want, if you don't share your goals with them. They may think they know what's best for you or they may simply want you to help them feel better about the decisions they've made (urging you to splurge on yourself, for example, to make them feel less guilty about spending too much on themselves). Unless you are clear about what your goals are and what you need from your loved ones in order to reach them, they can't help you.

I CAN SEE CLEARLY NOW
(Sandra)

The best part of the perfect day exercise for me was finally being able to see what I really wanted to do with my money. Immediately after I did the exercise, I asked myself: Why am I not living this day right now? Or, at the very least, why am I not taking the steps to get me to my perfect day? Did I really want to be spending so much on beauty products that I hardly ever used? Did I really want to pay $13 for parking every day? The answer, of course, was no! I wanted to be saving for things that really made me happy, and those "things" were staring right back at me in my perfect day. From that day forward, I consciously questioned every purchase that I made—asking, is this spending getting me anywhere closer to my perfect day? Friends at work would ask to go get a coffee, and I would gladly tag along for the walk and good gossip, but I passed on the coffee because I knew I would rather save that money for my condo (or maybe just for a jacket for the new season).

The perfect day exercise actually made me question a lot of aspects of my life—not just how I spent my money but also how I spent my time. I realized two things very quickly: first, that I cannot afford to not get paid what I am worth and, second, that I can't be working in a job that doesn't make me happy. It became clear to me that I wanted eventually to begin a business to help other women live a rich and fabulous life—a goal we realized we all shared. That prompted us to begin thinking about how we could make it happen together. I knew that I wasn't in a position to leave my current job right away, but I immediately put a plan into place that would allow me to leave as soon as possible and to earn more money to fund my dreams and enable me to work in my dream job.

Doing the perfect day exercise also helped me to stop being an instant gratification shopper. Being excited about saving money for the things in my perfect day makes it much easier to avoid those impulse purchases that used to drain all of my savings. Before, I knew that I needed to save, but it wasn't exciting to do so, because I didn't know what I was saving for. Now I know.

Of course, if you had the money to create your perfect day now, you probably wouldn't be reading this book. So the next step is to find out what's standing between you and the life you want. Is it credit-card debt, a lack of savings, or income that's just too low? Let's add it up.

Look at the three items that you listed in the perfect day exercise. Next to each item, write down about how much money you'd need to have it. This may require a little research. If it's a Mercedes convertible that you want, check the sticker price online (or look for a used version). If it's a three-bedroom home in a specific neighborhood, check your local real estate listings or call a realtor. If it's a baby, do a little research to find out whether your health insurance covers all the cost of pregnancy and delivery; how much child care costs in your city; and how much you'd need to pay for the basics in your baby's nursery. Several sites offer checklists of what you'll need for a baby, including: www.expectantmothersguide.com and www.babycenter.com. You can estimate prices by checking retailers with online sites like Target, Wal-Mart, Buy Buy Baby, and Babies R Us. And don't forget to check eBay and Craig's List (craigslist.org), which are often great, inexpensive sources for slightly used items that the seller's baby has outgrown. (We can't emphasize this enough: there is no shame in buying used—especially when it comes to kids, who outgrow toys and clothes long before they're worn out.) Babycenter also has a cost calculator for estimating how much it will cost you for the baby's first year at: http://www.babycenter.com/babyCostCalculator.htm. But it's realistic to expect that you'll be paying at least $10,000 that year, if you plan to use any sort of child care.

Don't be depressed if the prices seem out of reach now. In the next few chapters, we'll not only show you how to save more but how to make more money too. Smart Cookies don't just plan their perfect day, they plan *for* their perfect day so they can make it happen!

HOW WE DID IT
A Career Change
(Angela)

The perfect day exercise prompted some big life changes for me. After taking a good look at what I value most and what I want to have in my life, I realized that the job I had—though I really enjoyed it—was not going to get me to my "perfect day" anytime soon. My work schedule and salary were not allowing me to indulge in some of my favorite pastimes, like reading, traveling, and spending quality time with family and friends. I knew I needed more flexibility. I also realized after doing the exercise and discussing my dreams with the other Smart Cookies that I valued my independence in a career and also wanted a job that would provide unlimited earning potential. I wanted to be able to fund my big dreams like owning a beautiful home with a walk-in closet full of fabulous clothes, a tub built for two, and an incredible library filled with my favorite books, pictures, and possessions. I also wanted to own a family cottage near my hometown and to take a dream vacation to a spa in Arizona with my mom.

I was initially a bit hesitant about leaving my job. But I realized that I could have a different career that provided me with the same intangible rewards—and paid more! The overwhelming excitement I felt at the thought of what my life could be if I started making the moves in the right direction helped me overcome any fear or uncertainty I had about making the leap. After a lot of thought and with the support of the other Smart Cookies, I decided not only to change careers but to go into business for myself. I'll share more details in the upcoming chapters on how I did it, but I can tell you now that I am so glad I did. I love my new job as a realtor. It allows me to be creative, to meet lots of new people, and to feel as if I am improving their lives. And I am more confident now that I will be able to afford the life that I want. I've already started setting aside money for the major items in my perfect day.

THREE OF ANGELA'S BIG-TICKET ITEMS:

A vacation to Miraval Health Spa in Tucson, Arizona: A stay at the luxurious resort is expensive. But for a spa lover like her, it's the ultimate once-in-a-lifetime indulgence—especially if she can bring her mom along.

Estimated cost: $6,000 (for both of them).

How she came up with the price: Angela checked out the spa's website and price list and spoke to a representative by phone, then looked up airfares on various sites to get a range. The cost of a three-night stay for two people, including accommodation, meals, one spa service apiece, unlimited access to programs and activities, and transportation to and from the airport is about $5,000. The price of a round-trip ticket from where they live to Tucson, Arizona, ranges from about $250 to $400 apiece (so $500 to $800 for both of them). She also included $200 to pay for gifts or cover additional expenses.

How she'll get it: As a realtor, she saves 2.5 percent of every commission check for this trip, and any of the money she's earmarked for "fun" in her spending plan that she has left over at the end of the month goes toward this vacation. (After just two months, she had almost $500 saved already!) As she becomes more established in the real estate business and makes more money, the percentage she sets aside will increase to ensure that she will have the funds in time to reach her goal of visiting the spa in early 2010.

Complete wardrobe: Angela wants to expand her wardrobe so that she has several well-made pieces that she could wear for a long time and for a variety of occasions. She wants to have a closet full of beautiful clothes and accessories and feel really stylish and put together every day.

Estimated cost: $6,000 a year.

How she came up with the price: This is a ballpark estimate, but it comes out to about $1,500 a season, which should allow her to buy several expensive pieces that will last a long time and still have enough left over to add more trendy items and accessories. As she increases the number of basic quality items in her wardrobe, she figures she'll end up spending less as the seasons go by.

How she'll get it: She allows herself to spend $300 from every commission check on new items for her wardrobe. This goal has affected her everyday spending habits too, because she always thinks: If I don't go out to dinner or (fill in the blank), I can have another $50 for clothes! For a fashionista like her, the trade-off is worth it.

Family vacation home: Angela and her family have always dreamed of owning a beautiful lakefront cottage where they can meet several times a year. Her older brother and her sister-in-law are planning to split the cost with her. Hopefully, she will have a partner who is involved in the purchase as well.

Estimated cost: $600,000 ($300,000 for her, and $300,000 for her brother and sister-in-law).

How she came up with the price: When Angela was home for a visit this summer, she and her family toured some lakefront cottages they liked. She and her brother have since done some research and found cottages that fit their criteria that are around $600,000. Yes, that's a lot of money, and it will probably take them a while to save enough to buy a vacation home that expensive. But she says she doesn't feel discouraged by the price tag. If anything, she is more motivated than ever.

How she'll get it: Right now, eight percent of every commission check she gets goes toward funding this dream. Again, as she begins to build her business and is able to put more toward this investment, she certainly will.

Hidden Money

There are many different ways to save up for your big-ticket items. Sandra, one of the youngest among us and the one earning the smallest paycheck, managed to save or invest almost $8,000 in just one year by finding what we call "hidden money." Here's how she did it:

- She simplified her grocery shopping plan, shopping just once a week and limiting her weekly spending to $40 by buying simple, inexpensive items like bagels and cream cheese, sliced bread, canned tuna, and fruit. (She eats some meals out.) Savings: $180 a month.
- She started sharing and swapping clothes with friends. Savings: $250 a month.
- She moved in with a roommate. Savings: $400 a month.
- Total savings in one year = nearly $9,960 (enough to pay off her $2,000 debt and still save almost $8,000!).

Not all of your goals need to be financial. Katie had three specific personal goals that came from imagining her perfect day: to take at least a month each year to spend on vacations with her parents, grandparents, husband, and closest friends; to cook healthy dinners for herself and her husband at least three times a week; and to work out at least three times a week in the mornings. She set timelines for each. She wanted to be in a position by the summer of 2007 to take at least four weeks of vacation a year to spend time with her friends and family. Sure enough, by August, Katie had launched her own PR business and was in the position to decide how much vacation she wanted to take. She had also begun grocery shopping and regularly cooking dinners for herself and her husband, taking time to come up with healthier meals. And she'd set up an exercise routine so that she could work out at least three times a week.

Her financial goals also reflected her vision for her perfect day. She and her husband want to pay off the mortgage on their condo, then sell it and use the proceeds to help buy their dream home. Toward that end, they are consistently making extra payments on their mortgage. They're also setting aside savings for at least one indulgent vacation each year, besides trips to visit family or friends. (Next stop: the Bahamas.) Her final goal was to save some of the $250 she and her husband had allocated monthly for her clothes shopping so that she could splurge once a season on good-quality clothes. By cutting back a little each month on shopping now, she aims to have an extra $400 for fall 2008 wardrobe additions.

Using the estimates you wrote down, list three financial goals in your notebook that you want to accomplish over the next few years to help make your perfect day a reality. (You may want to list other nonfinancial goals as well.)

It's okay if they seem pretty unrealistic at this particular moment. At the time each of us came up with our financial goals, we weren't quite sure how we'd be able to accomplish them either. But as we created our spending plans and adjusted our habits, we actually started to see some real changes. In the months that followed, each of us made significant strides toward achieving the goals we'd written down. We'll help you do the same. It's possible to live your perfect day within the next few years if you start taking steps now.

Remember: Setting money aside for larger goals doesn't mean you can't have fun along the way. It's just a matter of prioritizing.

Once you commit yourself to setting money aside for the long-term goals that really matter to you, a funny thing happens. You'll begin to find that short-term spending (that is, spending that yields little return in the long run) becomes less appealing. You'll start looking at how you spend money in a whole new way, asking yourself if each purchase is *worth* your hard-earned money. Trust us. It will get easier to say no to $150 jeans or to a $45 meal tab if you know it means waiting that much longer to reach your bigger goals. This does not mean that you can't indulge occasionally in expensive clothes or a night out on the town with your friends. It's just a matter of where you want to put your money and when.

If you're a foodie who gets great pleasure out of feasting on an $85 prix fixe menu at a four-star restaurant, then do it! Just make sure it's an occasional treat and doesn't get in the way of your bigger goals. If spending more on a five-course meal means another month of saving to pay for the weeklong cooking course in Tuscany you've dreamed about, then you might want to reconsider and simply sample an appetizer and a drink at the restaurant's bar this time. If you're a fashionista who knows you'll wear those $150 jeans at least a couple of times a week, then using some of the money you set aside for clothes on one well-made, long-lasting pair of jeans may make more sense than spending the same amount on a half dozen trendy tops that might not last more than a season. (Of course, if you're like us, you probably don't really need another pair of jeans at all, and you might be better off putting that money into a savings account so you can earn interest on the $150 while you mull over future wardrobe additions.)

Think about some of your short-term and long-term goals. How much do you realistically think you'll need to achieve those goals? Which would you like to accomplish first?

Now take a good look at the work sheet on pages 28 to 31 that shows where your money has been going in a typical month. Do you notice categories—like cable or clothes shopping—where you'd prefer to spend less money? In some cases, you'll need to ask yourself tough questions and weigh your priorities. But it's likely that there are also areas where it won't be hard to cut your spending back right away—either because you've realized that you're not getting much of a return for the money you're spending or because you've come up with cheaper alternatives.

Andrea, for example, made a list of things she could live without or with less of and not feel deprived. On the list: her premium cable, daily Starbucks runs, dinners and drinks out with friends, and clothes. Next she started shopping around and brainstorming to come up with less expensive alternatives (another way to find "hidden money"). In the end she decided to just downsize her cable, switching to basic cable and changing providers so she'd get a better deal. The savings: $500 a year. She didn't want to cut out her Starbucks trips altogether, but she decided she could cut them in half and save as much as $75 a month. She invested in a $40 coffeemaker and now makes her coffee at home most days. She was okay with cutting down on expensive dinners, but she didn't want to spend less time with her friends, so they started hosting nights in instead. The $6 Girls' Night In was born. Each Smart Cookie would bring $6, and the combined $30 would cover a bottle (or two) of wine and some takeout or snacks. Andrea also stopped taking her car to the car wash and drove it to her parents' place on the weekend instead, then used their hose and cleaning supplies to wash it herself. This way she also had a chance to spend time with her family. Finally, she made note of a few boutiques where she consistently overspent and avoided them—or brought along one of us to talk her out of any impulse purchases. By cutting back a little in each area, she was able to save hundreds of dollars each month.

In your notebook, list at least five items you can cut or cut back on without feeling deprived. Now tally up how much you'll save by making those changes. Remember this number when you're tempted to overspend! And don't forget those goals.

The "Rather" Factor

We came up with the Rather Factor during one of our discussions about the social pressures and obligations that made it challenging for us to stick with our spending plans (which we'll help you create in the next chapter). Robyn was recounting at one meeting how she'd shelled out close to $100 recently on an expensive birthday dinner for a friend of a friend. She sighed and added that she would rather have put that money toward the trip she planned to take to Paris. And the Rather Factor was born.

As we mentioned earlier, we each realized that we'd been spending way too much money out of a sense of obligation, guilt, or social pressure, instead of spending money in ways that would bring us real satisfaction and fulfillment. Once we started paying attention, we were able to reallocate our spending to direct more toward the people and purchases that meant the most to us and to cut back on those obligations that often left us feeling frustrated at the amount of money we'd spent. We're not suggesting that you turn down every social invitation you get that's not from a close friend or family member, or bail on your boss's birthday lunch (that might not be good for your prospects at work), but instead of buying a $30 bottle of wine for your party host, pick up a small bouquet of flowers instead. They'll last longer and they'll be a nice reminder the day after the party of your thoughtfulness. Or, instead of dropping a lot of money on an expensive after-work meal with colleagues, join them for drinks and then skip out on dinner and save that money for a meal with a close friend or to put toward a larger goal. Or suggest a less expensive restaurant. You may find that your colleagues eagerly agree. Many of them are probably trying to save money as well and are happy to spend less of it on dinner. The reason you are going out in the first place is to spend time together socially, outside of work, so it should matter a lot less where you meet than that you can all enjoy it. (We'll share many more tips on cutting costs without cutting into your social life in the next chapter too.)

When an old colleague invited Katie to lunch recently, she suggested they get coffee or go for a walk instead, since she'd *rather* put that money toward the down payment on a house she and her husband are hoping to purchase soon. When Sandra was trying to pay off her credit-card balance of $2,000, she adopted a new mantra. Every time she went shopping with any of us and spotted a cute outfit she was tempted to buy, she'd remind herself and us: "No thanks, I would rather have a zero balance on my credit card than a new summer wardrobe." By the time the season was over, she'd paid off her debt and had a new appreciation for the clothes she already had in her wardrobe. And in an effort to support her goals—and to save money ourselves—we *all* agreed to share our clothes, since we're about the same size. When any of us had the urge to wear something new, we could just "shop" in one of the other Smart Cookies' closets.

Once you've identified a few areas where you can trim your spending, use your notebook to fill in the blanks below:

I'd rather have enough money to_____
than spend money on _____.

You can write out as many examples as you want. It's a good idea to also write these out on a slip of paper and then tape that to the first page of your notebook or—better yet—to the back of a credit card. That way, it will be there when you're tempted to use the card. It's amazing how much money you can redirect toward your goals just by keeping in mind what you'd rather spend your money on.

HOW WE DID IT

Angela was amazed at how easy it was for her to find "hidden money," just by deciding:

- She'd rather create an office space at home and have the money to travel to see her family in Toronto than rent desk space at the real estate office.
  Renting office space: $150/month.
  Total savings: $1,800 a year.
- She'd rather live in an inland apartment with two good friends for a year and save money than live alone in a condo close to the beach that charges a much higher rent.
  Former rent: $750/month.
  Current rent: $350/month.
  Total savings: $4,800 a year.

- She'd rather have drinks out with her girlfriends twice a month than buy her lunches daily.
Lunches/snacks monthly: $150.
Drinks out twice a month: $80.
Total savings: $840 a year.

Just by making these three choices, Angela saved nearly $7,500 in a year!

Robyn's goal was even more ambitious. She had a smaller salary as a social worker, yet she wanted to pay off a $5,000 balance on her credit card in one summer. And she did it. Here's how.

Step One:
Robyn's social work schedule allowed her a couple of short workdays but also kept her on the road for more than ten hours two days each week. She got used to taking her dog, Lucy, to doggy day care on the days she had to work late, at a cost of $200 a month. She wanted to save that money but she also wanted to make sure that her dog got enough exercise on the days she had to be at work for long stretches. So she worked out a plan with a friend in the neighborhood who also had a dog. They agreed to provide dog walking services for each other on alternate days. On two of the days that Robyn was home early, she would walk both her dog and her friend's dog; her friend returned the favor on days when Robyn worked late. (This could also be done with friends who have children and live near each other to save money on babysitting.) Savings: $600 over three months.

Step Two:
Robyn owned a parking spot that came with her town home, but there was also free parking in the street. She started parking her own car a bit farther away and renting out her parking spot. She only charged $50 a month, but it was a pretty effortless way to bring in a little extra money. Savings: $150 over three months.

Step Three:

She was still short $4,250—more than she could afford to cut from her spending. So she decided to look for additional freelance work. She called the professional association that represents social workers to inquire about contract jobs and learned of one particular project that paid $1,000 a month, plus two smaller jobs that would net her a combined $1,000 over the next three months. Then she turned these extra earnings into savings: $4,000.

Step Four:

Now she was down to just $250. She was nearly out of time and ideas when, with one month to go, a friend mentioned she needed a temporary place to stay while she looked for an apartment to buy. Robyn converted an alcove in her town home into an extra bedroom for her friend, who paid $350 a month in rent. Not only was that enough for Robyn to pay off the remaining balance on her card, but she had an extra $100 to spare.

Sticking to a spending plan isn't about telling your friends or yourself, "I can't afford (fill in the blank)." It's about making a conscious choice about how you want to spend your hard-earned money. No one wants to be the kind of person who adds up the bill at the end of a meal with friends, refusing to split the check since her entrée was $2 less than her friends'. And no one wants to be known as "cheap" or to miss out on invitations to dinner or to vacation with friends who assume you won't be interested because you're "on a budget." The fact is: You can still get vacation rentals with friends or splurge on an expensive dinner. It's *your* choice. You can cut back wherever you want, so that you have the money to do those things that are truly important to you. It is just a matter of prioritizing how you spend your money, not being cheap.

Rather than thinking about what you aren't buying now, remember to focus on what that money you saved will bring you later. The satisfaction you'll get from watching your savings grow (or your debt shrink) will far outweigh any temporary high you'd get from a short-term splurge. And so will the realization that you are firmly in control of your money, and each purchase you make—or don't make—is a conscious choice.

Smart Cookie Summary

Discussion Questions:

1. How is your life different than you'd imagined it would be at this age?
2. How do you envision your life in one year (or in five)?
3. What about your life now brings you the most and the least amount of joy?
4. What would you rather be spending more, or less, money on?
5. What would you rather be spending more, or less, time doing?

Smart Steps:

1. Describe in detail what your perfect day would include.
2. Name three activities you would be doing on your perfect day.
3. Name three things you would have on your perfect day that you don't have now.
4. Estimate the cost of those three items and use the numbers to come up with three financial goals.
5. Create a vision board using photos, cut-out words, and symbolic images that illustrate the life you want.

chapter 4

If the Shoe Fits, You Don't Have to Buy It

How to Be a Smart Spender

Overspending and continuous, uncontrollable use of credit is a common problem—so much so that it seems perfectly normal in our society today. Ask around. Chances are that all of your friends have debt in some form or another. We are a nation of consumers, encouraged from a young age to spend the money we make almost as soon as, or even before, we get it. And the proliferation of plastic has only exacerbated the problem. For the first time since the Great Depression, the Commerce Department reported that the U.S. savings rate in 2006 had fallen to *negative* one percent. That means the average American not only spent every cent she made after taxes were taken out but also dipped into her savings or borrowed money to cover purchases.

We were certainly guilty of that. Among the five of us, we had about 15 credit cards. That sounds like a lot, but here's the really scary thing: That's actually *below* average. (According to Federal Reserve Board data, the average U.S. cardholder has five credit cards.)

Fighting the urge to spend every cent we make *is* tough. We're up against some pretty powerful forces. It's easy to get swept up in our celebrity-obsessed consumer culture. We can't even turn on the TV or radio, or surf the web, without being besieged by images of models, musicians, or movie stars touting their favorite brands of makeup, clothes, or furnishings—few of which the average person can realistically afford. (And, incidentally, none of which the celebrities likely paid for themselves, since companies are only too happy to shower them with expensive gifts in the hopes that they'll be photographed wearing or using them.)

As soon as we buy one product, it seems like an even better, newer version is already on the shelves. It's not enough—if you are to believe advertisers—to simply have a cell phone or a television. If you want to stay current, you'll have to haul that big-screen television you bought last year onto the curb and put your money into a new high-definition plasma-screen TV and upgrade your plain old cell phone to an eight-gigabyte iPhone, on which you can e-mail photos or browse the web as you chat with your friends. (Good luck trying to stay focused on the conversation!) Of course, by next year, there'll be yet another model vying for your attention and your money. What if we all just held on to our cell phones, TVs, computers, or iPods until they stopped working? The manufacturers' sales would drop dramatically. So their marketing departments have to convince us that we need to replace our perfectly good gadgets by making us feel that they're no longer cool.

Retailers are also increasingly aggressive in the ways they push their products: tracking our purchases online, for example, and then sending us tailor-made "special offers" and notices via e-mail. Meanwhile, ads now blanket almost every inch of available space—from bathroom stalls to the back of airplane motion-sickness bags. And, if we want to get a good seat at the movie theater these days, we have to sit through fifteen minutes of commercials as well as fifteen minutes of previews!

Have you ever seen an ad encouraging you to *increase* your monthly credit-card payments so you can get out of debt faster? We'll bet you haven't. The more money you save or put toward your debt, the less money retailers or creditors can make off you. But we guarantee you've seen commercials for "debt management" firms that are happy to step in when you get overwhelmed—for a fat fee, of course.

There's a reason why personal bankruptcies hit an all-time high in 2005 and why nearly half of U.S. households carry a credit-card balance—on average about $5,100, according to the Federal Reserve Board's 2004 Survey of Consumer Finances. (Others claim the number is even higher—CardWeb.com, which tracks credit-card trends, says the average credit-card debt among households with at least one credit card was more than $8,900 in 2002.) By this spring, the total U.S. consumer debt had soared to nearly $2.56 trillion—a record-high $957 billion of that revolving debt, like credit cards and home equity lines of credit, according to the Federal Reserve. Women, specifically, seem to be spending a lot more than we're making. Not only are we more likely to go bankrupt (in 2005, an estimated 150,000 more women than men filed for bankruptcy in the United States), but we are also more likely than men to carry consumer credit-card debt, according to the *Journal of Financial Planning*. Men, on the other hand, are more likely to take on debt to start a small business or to invest—both of which are likely to yield higher returns than that $300 Kate Spade bag you bought on credit, then sold on eBay two years later for less than half the price.

Even our political leaders aren't exactly the best role models for fiscal responsibility. The U.S. budget deficit hit an all-time high in 2004 of $413 billion—or about $1,410 *per person* living in America. (It has since declined, but not by much: It was expected to be about $396 billion for the fiscal year ending September 30, 2008, according to the Congressional Budget Office.) Even as millions of Americans struggle to keep up with debt payments, the government urges us on, claiming that shopping is patriotic because it contributes to the country's economy. What did President George W. Bush encourage Americans to do when the economy stalled after the 9/11 terror attacks? Shop! And when the country teetered on the brink of recession in early 2008, Congress approved tax rebates for millions of Americans, with the intention that most of that money would be spent. When President Bush announced the rebates, he even said: "When the money reaches the American people, we expect they will use it to boost consumer spending." (Consumer spending does account for nearly 70 percent of the country's Gross Domestic

Product. But that doesn't mean you should spend more the next time you hit the mall out of patriotic duty. Use your savings to buy a home instead—that's good for the economy *and* your financial well-being.)

Women seem particularly susceptible to messages encouraging us to spend, perhaps because so often they appear to be aimed at us. (Advertisers do recognize that women are the primary decision-makers for household spending.) Think of the Visa ad from 2007 that featured a woman having a horrible day—she's caught in the rain and the heel of her shoe breaks. Then a stranger, a fairy godmother of sorts, whisks her off to a salon and a shoe store and, thanks to her Visa, she and her day are completely transformed. Of course, they don't show her the day her billing statement arrives!

We're constantly urged by advertisers—and even by some so-called financial experts—to spend money to improve our wardrobes, our appearance, and our self-esteem because "we're worth it!" But do you really want to measure your worth by how much you spend on material goods? That's a dangerous, not to mention costly, proposition. And it can leave you like Carrie Bradshaw in the episode of *Sex and the City* we discussed earlier: with a closet full of fabulous clothes and shoes, a bunch of maxed-out credit cards, and so little savings in your account that the bank wouldn't even consider giving you a mortgage. Talk about a dwindling sense of worth.

Even the way we *make* purchases allows us to perpetuate the cycle of denial.

In 2003, for the first time in history, shoppers began using plastic (credit and debit cards) more than cash. The volume of debit-card transactions in the U.S. has more than tripled since 2000, while credit-card transactions grew by about 50 percent in the same period. There's nothing wrong with using a debit card, because you need to have money in your checking account to cover your purchase. It sure beats a credit card. But when you pull out plastic in any form, you're much less likely to think about how much money you're actually spending. How many times have you gone to the supermarket with a debit card to pick up a few things for dinner and ended up with a $50 bill and a fridge full of groceries you didn't intend to buy? You figure, well, you're putting it all on your card anyway—why not stock up? Plus, it seems silly to use a debit card to pay for one tiny purchase, so it's tempting to add more to make it seem worth it. Some retailers actually require a $10 or $20 minimum purchase now (mainly because they're charged processing fees each time customers use their debit or credit cards). Bring cash instead—especially a set amount like $20—and we guarantee that you'll be much less likely to keep adding items to your cart impulsively because: a) you don't want to be embarrassed at the register when you realize you're a couple bucks short, and b) it's human nature to want to hold on to some of that cash when you leave the store. There's something painfully real about handing over a crisp $20 bill and getting just a few coins in return.

If our parents spent too much, the check would bounce. Or they'd simply run out of cash before the next paycheck arrived and have to go without. But with credit cards, overdraft protection, and online bill payments that simply subtract the minimum payments from our accounts without reminding us of the balance owed, many of the external reality checks that used to exist have disappeared. It's become dangerously easy to overspend without any major repercussions—well, until the pink slip, eviction notice, or collection agency's letter arrives. By then it's too late.

If we want to be financially successful, we have to stop thinking of ourselves as just consumers and start thinking of ourselves as savers and investors, even if advertisers and credit-card companies are doing everything they can to convince us otherwise.

What Kind of Spender Are You?

We're not asking you to stop spending money, just to be smarter about how you spend it. First, it's important to identify and acknowledge your weak spots so you can take steps immediately to avoid potentially treacherous situations that will have you spending money for all the wrong reasons. Maybe you're the type of person who feels tempted to buy anything that's on sale for fear of missing out on a bargain, like Katie, or who goes to the grocery store to pick up one item and ends up with a cart full of stuff she couldn't resist buying, like Angela. Or you feel compelled to buy something for yourself if you're having a bad day, like Robyn. For many people, spending is guided as much by instinct and emotion as by reason. So if you want to change your habits, you need to know what drives them.

Can you go for days without spending much money, then blow all you've saved up in one outing? Do you willingly pay more for milk or orange juice at the convenience store around the corner just because you don't feel like driving or walking to a cheaper store that is farther away? All of us have been guilty of that sometimes. But once you become conscious of it, it's easier to find the motivation to walk a little farther to save more money. In fact, once you've figured out your spending patterns, you'll become much more aware of overspending merely out of boredom, laziness, sadness, or peer pressure—any number of reasons that don't make sense. And it will be that much easier to stop.

To help you identify what influences your spending, rank each of the statements below from 1 to 5, circling the number that best applies to you. Then tally your score to find out what kind of spender you are.

1 = never, 2 = rarely, 3 = sometimes, 4 = usually, 5 = always.

1. I can go weeks without spending a dime on clothes, then drop $500 during one afternoon shopping spree.
    1 2 3 4 5

2. If I spend too much on a night out with my friends, I'll drastically cut my spending the next day to make up for it.
    1 2 3 4 5

3. I'll suffer buyer's remorse after a really big purchase and force myself to return the item.
    1 2 3 4 5

4. I'll be really responsible about saving money for a while, then "reward" myself by splurging on a big purchase.
    1 2 3 4 5

5. I'd rather spend $1 more for a gallon of milk at the convenience store if it will save me a longer trip to the grocery store.
    1 2 3 4 5

6. I use my debit card because I don't feel like going to the ATM for cash.
    1 2 3 4 5

7. I wouldn't pick up take-out food when I can get it delivered.
    1 2 3 4 5

8. I like to buy lunch at the restaurant that's closest to my office—it's more expensive, but it's also more convenient than other places.
    1 2 3 4 5

9. When I'm depressed, I'll take myself out for a "treat"—a massage or some new clothes—to boost my mood.
    1 2 3 4 5

10. I've gone shopping with friends and then been surprised later when I looked at the receipt and realized how much I spent.
    1 2 3 4 5

11. If I see something I like, I tend to buy it—no matter what the price tag.
    1 2 3 4 5

12. I make a shopping list before I go to the grocery store, but I end up buying almost as many things that aren't on the list.
    1 2 3 4 5

13. If I see the words "sale" or "discount," I allow myself to buy more.
    1 2 3 4 5

14. I'm willing to splurge on an expensive pair of shoes if they're marked down from the original price.
    1 2 3 4 5

15. I find myself explaining, "But they were on sale!"
1 2 3 4 5

16. I've bought clothes from the bargain bins even though I wasn't sure I'd ever wear them.
1 2 3 4 5

17. I've put items into my shopping cart at the grocery store and then wondered later why I picked them up.
1 2 3 4 5

18. I don't look at the price of the entrées when I order from a restaurant menu.
1 2 3 4 5

19. When I see the receipt after checking out at the grocery store, I am completely surprised by how high the total is.
1 2 3 4 5

20. I've spent more than I intended during a night out and wondered where the money went.
1 2 3 4 5

21. I don't need to have a lot of clothes, but having designer labels is important to me.
1 2 3 4 5

22. I would rather charge a Prada bag on my credit card than buy a cheap knockoff with cash.
1 2 3 4 5

23. I'd spend a little more for a designer shirt, even if the label only appears on the inside.
1 2 3 4 5

24. I often find myself arguing, "But everyone's wearing them!"
1 2 3 4 5

(Remember: 1 = never, 2 = rarely, 3 = sometimes, 4 = usually, 5 = always.)

Look below to see what type of spender you are. (And, yes, it's possible to be more than one kind.) You don't need to answer "always" to exhibit tendencies toward a certain type of spending pattern. This assessment is meant to serve as a guide, so that you're more aware of the reasons you may overspend.

If your total score for questions 1 through 4 was 12 points or higher:

You're a Yo-Yo Spender, depriving yourself some days, then overcompensating on other days, depending on your mood, and hoping it will all even out in the end. Too bad it doesn't work that way. Bingeing and purging isn't good for your diet or your wallet!

If your total score for questions 5 through 8 was 12 points or higher:

You're a Slacker Spender. To you, convenience often matters more than cost. You're more likely to buy your clothes at the boutique near your office than trek across town to the outlet stores. If the cheaper plane ticket requires a stopover or an early-morning takeoff, you'll gladly pay more to sleep in and take a nonstop flight. In some cases, convenience may be worth the cost. But, often, just a little extra effort could result in some big savings.

If your total score for questions 9 through 12 was 12 points or higher:

You're an Impulse Spender. For you, emotion trumps reason when it comes to spending money. It's for people like you that grocery stores line the shelves of the checkout lanes with candy and toiletries and magazines, betting that you won't be able to resist picking up one last thing while you're waiting to reach the register.

If your total score for questions 13 through 16 was 12 points or higher:

You're a "Sale!" Spender. The words "sale" and "discount" and "clearance" make you reach instinctively for your wallet, even if you spend more than you intended (hey, you're still getting a bargain, right?). Your instincts are right. The problem is that the discount item may not even be something you need. If you're never going to wear the shirt you bought on sale, then it's not much of a bargain at any price.

If your total score for questions 17 through 20 was 12 points or higher:

You're a Zombie Spender, paying little attention to where your money goes. You can come home from the grocery store and wonder why—or when—you picked up some of the items in your bags. You often end up with less money in your wallet than you thought you had but aren't sure where it went. When you spend money without thinking about it, it's very easy to overspend.

If your total score for questions 21 through 24 was 12 points or higher:

You're a Status Spender, and you wouldn't dream of cutting corners with cheap knockoffs. You're an avid reader of *Vogue* and can effortlessly tick off the latest fashion trends and hottest designers. For you, the brand matters more than the price. If only your income was as good as your sense of style! Good thing there are sample sales, eBay, online discounters selling brand names, and friends' closets to raid. Now you just need to take advantage of those less expensive options.

Taking this quiz forced each of us to confront our spending habits. Sandra wasn't the only one guilty of plunking down a lot of money on one shopping trip. Andrea realized that she was both a Yo-Yo Spender—trying to offset a $500 shopping spree one day by canceling plans the next day to save money—and a Slacker Spender. When she was feeling lazy, she admitted to us, she'd often have take-out food delivered, even from the restaurant that was just across the street. She was essentially paying extra for the delivery (in tips) just so she didn't have to muster up the energy or effort to get dressed and go outside. On the other hand, she found one advantage to her slacker tendencies: Sometimes she would put off a purchase for so long because she didn't feel like schlepping to the store that her desire to have that item eventually went away and she ended up saving herself the trip, and the money! Now, there's one benefit we had not considered.

Katie found her splurges were usually tied to being a Sale Spender, though she had Status Spender tendencies too (with 11 points). After she took the quiz, she laughed as she recounted a perfect example that had happened just a couple of evenings before, when she went to the drugstore to pick up some toothpaste, shampoo, and conditioner. Just as she was reaching for the hair products she typically uses, she noticed a 2-in-1 product containing both shampoo and conditioner that was marked down to 99 cents. She ended up buying three bottles, simply because it was "too good a deal to resist," even though she admitted she doesn't like 2-in-1 products and wasn't likely to use them. There's an important lesson there. Discounts and sales are great. And sometimes it's worth replacing a product you typically use, if you can save a lot of money on a different brand. But if you don't *use* the product that you bought on sale, it's not a good deal no matter what the price. Katie ended up going back to the store to buy her usual shampoo and conditioner (fortunately, her husband was willing to try the 2-in-1 product, so those bottles didn't go to waste).

Robyn realized she was both a Yo-Yo and an Impulse Spender: a dangerous but not unusual combination. She recalled that when she consciously wanted to save money, she would cut back her spending for several weeks and be able to save an impressive amount. But then she would "reward" herself with a vacation, or another expensive purchase, and blow right through all that money she'd carefully set aside. She followed the same pattern with her clothes shopping—waiting two months sometimes to buy something new and then spending hundreds of dollars in one afternoon at the mall. Her impulse to splurge on herself was especially strong after breakups or other emotionally trying times. After her divorce, she splurged on three extravagant trips in one year, including a month-long trip to Thailand, and she spent thousands of dollars on new clothes. (This might help explain the five-figure debt she had when she joined the money group.)

Sandra racked up the most points as a Status Spender, which didn't surprise her. Even now, she says, she always prefers to spend a little more money on a brand she likes. But she's careful to choose items that will last a long time. Last fall, instead of buying two generic sweaters that she liked but didn't love for a combined $100, she opted to buy just one handmade sweater that she really loved for about the same price. Sure, she was getting one less sweater for her money, but she insisted she would hold on to this one for years and she knew she couldn't wait to wear it during the winter. Of course, this isn't an excuse to spend more on one item. But if you have a set amount of money, whether you choose to buy one relatively expensive handmade sweater or two retail chain store sweaters is up to you. If you're like Sandra, having a big wardrobe may be less important than having fewer but better-made clothes.

Sandra was surprised, though, to realize that her quiz responses also indicated she did a lot of Zombie spending. She'd always thought of herself as being a conscious spender, but she realized that when she was entertaining or out with friends, she often paid little attention to how much she spent (especially after a glass or two of wine). As a consequence, she sometimes overspent without being aware of where the money had gone. After taking the quiz, she resolved to become much more conscious about her money when she was out socializing. One solution: Figure out ahead of time about how much money you plan to spend when you go out, and put only that amount in your wallet. This way, you're less tempted to overspend. Knowing you'll have to find an ATM, borrow money, or pull out your debit or credit card can be enough to keep you within your limits.

Angela wasn't as surprised when she scored highest as a Zombie Spender. When she moved in to a new apartment, Angela went to IKEA with the intention of picking up just a few furnishings. Instead, she spent an afternoon walking up and down the aisles, adding any item that drew her attention to her shopping cart. When she got home, she realized she'd paid so little attention to what she was picking up that she'd bought not one but *three* different covers for her duvet! She's recalled other instances as well when she was forced to return items she'd bought and then realized she didn't need or already had in her closet. Not only was that a big time and energy drainer, but she wasn't always able to get a refund, so it was costing her money as well. That might explain why she also scored high for Yo-Yo spending: She often suffered buyer's remorse for big purchases and, if she couldn't return it for a refund, effectively punished herself by drastically cutting her spending for the next week or two to compensate. That's no fun! Better to be aware of what you're buying at the time, so you can return unneeded items to the shelf *before* you get to the cash register. Then you'll save yourself both money and regrets.

Arm Yourself with a Plan

No matter what kind of spender you are, you can come up with a new spending plan that is in line with both your financial goals and values. Take a look at the work sheet on pages 89 to 90. This is a lot like the sheet from Chapter Two in which you filled out how much you're now spending on bills and purchases, but we're going to use this one to create a spending plan that reflects your goals, values, and priorities. You'll see columns for two months with space for both estimated numbers and actual numbers. This plan will be used to fill in what you want to spend, save, invest, and pay toward your debts in the future—and what you *actually* spend, save, invest, and pay toward your obligations in the months ahead. For your long-term plan, you can either make a few photocopies of this or you can download a 12-month plan from our website.

Start by writing down how much you want to save each month, how much you want to put toward your debt, if you have any, and how much you want to put into investments. We'll help you decide how to invest your money for the best returns in Chapter Seven. But for now it's important just to get used to setting aside a specific amount each month for your future.

Next, write down how much you spend monthly on your rent or mortgage and nonnegotiable expenses like water, utilities, phone (cell and/or landline). Keep in mind that there are ways to cut some of those bills. (We've got several tips listed later in this chapter.)

You'll also notice a line marked "Fun Money." This is your guilt-free spending money. It's intended to go toward day-to-day activities or incidentals that aren't covered in your spending plans—from a concert with friends to a bag of candy for your office drawer. So you can either use it toward things that don't fall under a regular category (say, Groceries) in the spending plan or you can use the money to cover extras (like gourmet groceries from a specialty store) that would push you above the amount you'd allocated in that category. The point is: You can spend it on anything you want without having to justify it. If you're feeling the urge to splurge on a great new accessory, for example, but you've already used up the money for shopping that you set aside, you can tap into your fun money. Or use it to treat yourself and a friend to dinner, to indulge in a one-hour massage, a month's worth of mocha lattes—or even a designer dog leash.

The Smart Cookies have allowed ourselves $100 a week in fun money, though you can choose any amount you want. Each Sunday, we take that money out of our account and put it in an envelope. We can spend it on music or accessories or hardcover books or a couple of bottles of expensive wine—whatever we want. Robyn often saves her fun money up and then buys one expensive item of clothing. Andrea usually uses it for coffee drinks or cocktails with friends during the week. Angela likes to grab some of her fun money and then wander the aisles at the drugstore, filling her cart with magazines, lip gloss, nail polish, and any inexpensive item that happens to catch her eye. We found that having a little extra money set aside to use for whatever we felt like buying helped each of us stick to our spending plans without feeling deprived and allowed us to indulge in the occasional impulse purchase or big night out without getting off track financially. The only rule is that once it's gone, we have to wait until the next week to refill the fund, and there's no resorting to debit or credit cards in the meantime.

Now, with the money that's left from your earnings, fill in the remaining blanks for discretionary expenses like clothes, meals out, etc. Don't fret if the numbers look low. We're going to show you how you can stretch each dollar to get the most for your money. You'll be paying a lot less, but you'll hardly notice the difference in your life or your wardrobe!

Living Large on Less

Saving money for the future you want doesn't mean feeling guilty about every cent you spend on yourself now. Who would want to stick to a plan that entails that much suffering?

SPENDING PLAN

	Month 1 / Est.	Month 1 / Act.	Month 2 / Est.	Month 2 / Act.
INCOME				
Wages				
Extra Earnings				
INCOME TOTALS				
EXPENSES				
Utility Bills				
Maintenance				
Cable/Internet				
Cellular Telephone				
Home Telephone				
Water Bill				
Home Repairs/Decor				
Groceries				
Meals Out				
Gas				
Car Insurance				
Public Transportation				
Parking				
Gym Membership				
Health Insurance				
Life Insurance				
Home Insurance				
Misc. Spending				
Clothing				
Entertainment				
Fun Money				
Other				
EXPENSES/SPENDING TOTAL				

SPENDING PLAN (continued)

	Month 1 / Est.	Month 1 / Act.	Month 2 / Est.	Month 2 / Ac
SAVINGS				
Investments				
Savings Account				
SAVINGS TOTAL				
MONEY OWED				
Credit Cards (or Credit Line)				
Car Loan				
Student Loans				
Mortgage/Rent				
MONEY OWED TOTAL				
TOTAL EARNINGS				
TOTAL EXPENSES				
CASH LEFT				

The Smart Cookies are all about preserving the lifestyle you enjoy—just doing it for less. Each of us managed to find lots of ways we could save extra money, without feeling like we were giving up the things that gave us pleasure. When it comes to deciding what spending strategies work best for you, it's important to come up with some that fit with your lifestyle, not just your goals. We're not asking you to stop visiting the spa or to swap your cashmere sweater for a polyester blend just because it's cheaper. The idea is to figure out what is really important to you and what's not. We learned that we all spent a lot of money on things that didn't provide a great deal in return. And even in those areas that are important to us, there were ways to save money without sacrificing our social lives, stylish wardrobes, or the small luxuries that brighten our days.

Some places to look should be obvious to you by now. If you haven't watched HBO in more than six weeks, maybe it's time to consider switching to standard cable. If you're spending a disproportionate amount of your paycheck on dinners out, try meeting your friends for brunch or a drink instead. There are lots of easy ways to cut back a little without lowering your standard of living. Here are a few more of our personal favorites:

SOCIALIZING:

- Instead of meeting a girlfriend for dinner, suggest meeting for breakfast, lunch, or even coffee, as we mention above. If you eat out, dinner is always the priciest meal. And you are likely to have just as much fun no matter when or where you meet a friend. If you're dying to check out an expensive new restaurant, why not go early for a drink and split an appetizer? You'll get to sample the ambience and the menu for a fraction of the cost.
- Have a Girls' Night *In:* Rather than going out for dinner with your girlfriends, have $6 Girls' Nights In. Each person can spend $6 on food made for sharing—like pita bread, olives, and a container of hummus, for example, or a small pizza—and bring a regifted wine

smart **SC** bite

NEED SOME HELP FINDING THAT HIDDEN MONEY?
Here's a list of five seemingly small daily purchases that can add
up to a lot, along with a few options that will leave you with extra
money in your pocket:

1. Coffee: Yes, we've mentioned this before, and we're not saying
    you should go without your daily java, but do the math. There's
    a reason why personal finance guru David Bach's "Latte Factor"
    became a household term. If you get a $3.50 specialty coffee
    every day, that adds up to nearly $1,300 a year! Just by substi-
    tuting it with a regular $1.50 cup of coffee on weekdays and
    saving the lattes for weekends, when you can linger over them,
    you could save more than $500 a year.

2. Drinks: Even if you go out only on weekend nights and stick with a
    couple of glasses of reasonably priced wine (say, $8 a glass, includ-
    ing tip), you're still spending more than $1,650 on alcohol a year—
    and that's not including weekday outings. (If you live in a major
    city like New York, you can expect to pay even more. A glass of wine
    in a mid-priced Manhattan restaurant can cost $11 or more, not
    including tip.) Again, we're not advising that you stay home or stick
    to water, but you can save a lot by scheduling a Girls' Night *In* one

or combine funds with others to buy a bottle. We estimate that we
collectively saved at least $3,600 just by doing this once or twice a
week for one year. (How? We figured that we each would have
spent at least $20 had we gone out instead. So we took that $14
saved, multiplied it by 52, then by 5, the number of Cookies in our
money group.)

weekend night and sharing the cost of a bottle or two of inexpensive wine, for example, or by getting your drinking and socializing in early on Friday to take advantage of happy-hour specials.

3. Bottled water: A big bottle can average about $1.50. That adds up to nearly $550 a year, if you're buying water daily. It's really easy to cut that cost—and do your part for the environment— by buying one bottle and then refilling it at the office water cooler (or with your own filtered water).

4. Vending-machine snacks: You're at work, it's three o'clock, and you've got the munchies. But you don't have time to leave the office for a bite. So you head to the vending machine. Do this daily and it can add up to more than $250 a year (assuming your snack is about $1)—not to mention the extra, often empty, calories. Vending-machine snacks aren't good for your waist-line or your wallet. Pack a snack instead.

5. Weekday lunches out: This was one we all cut back on. Even if you're just running out for a sandwich and chips or a drink, you could easily end up spending $7 or more on lunch. That adds up to about $1,800 a year! If you spend $15 a week on bread, lunch meat, veggies, and condiments instead and make your own sandwiches, you could save $1,000 a year.

- Be fashionably late. Eat dinner at home before you go out to meet your friends. Then you can snack on an appetizer or skip the meal altogether and just have a drink or two with your friends.
- Eat early. Most restaurants and bars have happy-hour specials between the hours of five and seven p.m. on weekdays, with drinks at half price and a range of menu items for under $10. Why not meet a

friend right after work for a half-price drink and appetizer and then head home for dinner?

BEAUTY AND BODY MAINTENANCE:

- Exercise with friends. Health clubs are expensive. Many cost more than $1,000 a year and often require a commitment of a year or more. Gyms count on the likelihood that most members stop going, at least regularly, after a few weeks or months but are still stuck paying monthly dues until their contract runs out. Before you join a gym, consider organizing a group of friends for daily or weekly walks, runs, hikes, or bike rides instead. This way you can be social and be fit—and working out with friends will give you added incentive to stick to your exercise regime. If it's too cold or too hot where you live to exercise outside regularly, consider joining a Y, where the membership rates are often significantly lower than those at a higher-end health club.
- Make the most of municipal facilities. Most cities have free or discounted access to tennis courts, swimming pools, and other sports facilities. Check to see where you can play for less. Some cities even offer free use of boats at city-owned lakes and/or free (or discounted) rentals of golf clubs and use of the range or course at city-owned facilities.
- Let your hair down. Stretch out the time between haircuts. If you usually get your hair cut once every six weeks, try stretching it to once every eight weeks and save yourself the cost of at least two haircuts plus tips each year. If you color your hair, use a base color but skip highlights, which are costly and more damaging to your hair anyway.
- Dye it yourself. Yes, it's best to leave complicated hair-color jobs, like bleaching, to the pros. But if you're just covering gray roots or experimenting with a deeper shade of brown, you can buy good temporary, semipermanent, or permanent hair color at your local drugstore for a fraction of the cost of getting it colored in the salon.

- Shop at the drugstore, not the mall, for your beauty products. Some of the most effective and popular products can be found at your local drugstore for a lot less—from Maybelline's Great Lash, which is often cited as a top brand among models and makeup artists, to Oil of Olay's Regenerist, which was ranked as the most effective antiwrinkle cream by *Consumer Reports* in its January 2007 issue, even though it was the least expensive brand tested. (Of course, the cheapest and safest way to keep wrinkles at bay is to buy sunscreen and to avoid the sun. *Consumer Reports* found that the top performers reduced the average depth of wrinkles by less than ten percent, on average, after 12 weeks—barely enough to be detected by the naked eye.)

- Get made up for less. Take advantage of the free makeovers offered at makeup counters and boutiques before a big night out. And don't feel pressured to buy. If you like the results, you can just make note of the blush, eye shadow, eye liner, and lipstick colors that were used. Then go to your drugstore and look for cheaper makeup brands in the same shades. Or if you have a friend who always looks great, ask if she'd be willing to share her secrets and/or make you over one afternoon.

- Paint your own nails between pedicures. We wouldn't recommend that you give up pedicures and manicures altogether. It's nice to be pampered occasionally. But instead of spending $20 to $40 for a new paint job in a salon every time your nail polish chips, buy an extra bottle of the color polish that your salon used and do the touch-ups yourself. This way you can stretch out your time between visits to the salon and still have fabulous nails.

SAVING AT HOME:

- Talk less. If you don't use your cell phone that often, see if there's a cheaper monthly calling plan that allows fewer minutes. Compare rates, not just between packages but between service providers.

- Lose the landline. If you use your cell phone a lot, ask yourself if you really need a landline. If you still want phone service at home, consider switching to an Internet Phone Service (or VoIP). These providers route your calls through your high-speed broadband Internet connection, not a phone line. The quality is comparable but the cost is usually much lower than regular phone service. (Check out nextadvisor.com for a comparison of different VoIP services.)

- Cut the cable. Do you really need *all* of those cable channels? You could save a lot of money and maybe free up some time by just using basic cable. By giving up cable, Sandra saved both money—$900 a year!—and time. She used the time she once spent sitting in front of the TV to exercise, read, or hang out with friends, activities that proved to be more fulfilling to her than staring at a screen.

- Go paperless. Read your favorite newspaper online instead of subscribing. Or go to aggregate news sites like Google News, where you can read articles from publications all over the globe for free. Many magazines are also starting to post much of their content online for free.

- Be energy efficient. Turn off the lights when you leave a room. Turn the thermostat up in the summer or down in the winter when you're not home. Try a fan and open a window before resorting to the air conditioner. Unplug appliances when they're not in use. Switch to energy-efficient bulbs. Not only will you be saving money on your electric bill, but you'll be helping the environment too.

- Buy in bulk. Cut down on grocery costs by shopping once a week (where you can load up at a large discount store like Costco) instead of picking up a few items every day at the nearest shop. *Always* bring a list when you shop so you don't get sucked into making impulse purchases. And try not to shop when you're hungry and may be tempted by every delicious display.

- Decorate creatively. You can save money by printing out photos you like from the Internet, or photos you've taken, and having them framed instead of buying prints. Or go to a fabric store and buy a piece you like and have it framed. Pick up candles and knickknacks from discount stores or flea markets to add a personal touch. Try craigslist.org, the classifieds, or yard sales to find gently used furniture at great discounts. You can always buy a slipcover for the couch if its color doesn't match your decor—and for a lot less than it'd cost to buy a brand-new couch.

SHOPPING:

- Check for discounted display items. When we are making a major purchase, we always ask the salesperson if the store has any of last year's items on sale or if there's a display or demo model for sale. This works for cars, appliances, mattresses, furniture, and almost any big-ticket item. You would be surprised at how much you can save.

- Froogle it. Before you buy something, type it into Froogle.com to see if the item is available for a lower price. Froogle is Google's comparison shopping search engine—an easy way to compare different retailers' prices for the same item.

- Shop in-store then buy online. Last summer Sandra wanted two new pairs of high-end jeans. She went to Neiman Marcus and tried on the style and size that she wanted, then she went on to eBay, found exactly what she wanted, and paid $200 for *three* pairs of jeans that would have cost a lot more at the mall.

- Prowl the web for promo codes. Once you've filled your shopping cart at an online retailer, open another window and type the name of the retailer and "coupon" or "promo code" into your favorite search engine. You should be able to find discounts or coupons that you can use when you check out—saving as much as 30 percent or more.

- Carry the card. If you regularly shop at a particular store, see if they offer a frequent-shopper card. You can join for free and receive coupons (via mail or e-mail) and qualify for special discounts. Some stores give out coupons worth a specific cash amount off your next purchase once you've spent a certain amount of money there over time (for example: for every $100 you spend, regardless of how many separate trips it takes to reach that amount, you'd get a $5 off coupon to use within a certain period of time).

- Sign up for sale updates. Most clothing stores and boutiques now send out regular e-mail alerts to customers on their mailing lists about sales and special events. It takes two minutes to sign up, but the savings can be substantial. Another bonus: You can often plan ahead once you know when your favorite stores' regular sales are, so you can save up your money and then stock up on some of your favorite looks for less.

- Buy some time. If you're planning to shop in the same mall or retail area for a while, put the item you're considering on hold for a few hours. Then walk around before you decide whether to go back to the store and buy it. Once you're out of the environment and have had some time to think about your purchase, you may decide you can easily live without it.

- Scour secondhand stores. Thrift stores, "vintage" stores, and other secondhand shops are often treasure troves for the savvy shopper. Sure, you have to do some digging, but you can often find designer clothes and accessories at deeply discounted prices. Better yet, drop off some of your gently worn clothes, and you may get an even trade or come home with some extra money as well as extra clothes.

- Go generic. Most grocery stores offer generic or store brand versions of everything from cocoa to cookies, even diapers and baby wipes. Often the quality is comparable; the generic or store-brand versions are just less expensive because they don't spend much on design or marketing. If you pay out of pocket for medicine, you should also check regularly to see if generic versions of your prescription drugs are available yet. Under law, pharmaceutical companies must allow generic versions of their brand-name drugs to be sold after a certain period of time has elapsed. (Many health insurance companies now routinely require the use of generics, unless otherwise prescribed, in order to cut costs.)

Be a Fashionista (for Less)

It was essential to each of us that we not sacrifice our style for our savings or vice versa, and we've spent a lot of time brainstorming strategies to keep both our wardrobes and our wallets well stocked. In addition to the general advice listed in the section above, we've outlined our top ten tips below to help you stay fashionable *and* financially savvy:

1. **Take inventory of your closet quarterly**: The change in seasons is the perfect time to take stock of what you have in your wardrobe. You're going to be rearranging your closet anyway, so why not assess each item as you do? Is it in good condition? Are you still excited to wear it? Is it still stylish or is it out of date? Does it feel fashionable or frumpy? Your responses will help you decide what to do with it.

2. **Clear out the clutter**: As you're going through your clothes, shoes, and accessories, organize them into five piles: Save (split into two: As Is and Needs Work), Sell, Dump, or Donate. Hold on to only those items that still make you feel fashionable when you wear them. Some may need mending or updating; those go in the Needs Work pile. (Maybe a button came loose from a favorite blouse, or a heel needs to be replaced on one of your boots. These are easy fixes that don't require a lot of money.) Sell items that are expensive or well-made but don't get you excited about wearing them anymore. You can post them on eBay or craigslist.org or bring them to a consignment or secondhand shop. Dump those that have large holes or have been worn so much that they're not worth salvaging. If an item of clothing really has sentimental value—like an old concert T-shirt or a sweater that your grandmother made for you—consider saving a patch of it in a jewelry box or scrapbook instead of

letting it clutter up your closet. And donate clothing that's out of date but in good condition or doesn't fit you anymore. (There are plenty of worthy organizations that accept gently used clothing, like the Salvation Army, Goodwill Industries, and some Big Brother Big Sister facilities. You can donate shoes to Soles4Souls, a nonprofit that collects them for children and adults in need.) You won't get

smart SC bite

DONATE AND DEDUCT: While donating your old clothes and shoes helps, it's wonderful—and tax deductible—to support your favorite causes financially too. Just be aware that you won't be able to deduct cash donations unless you have a bank statement, a canceled check, or a receipt from the charity that proves you gave the amount you're claiming. And keep in mind that you can have a larger impact (and a smaller stack of follow-up requests in the mail) if you give more money or donations to fewer groups. Check out the organizations before you write a check or drop off your donation. Look for charities that have been granted tax-exempt status under section 501(c)(3) of the IRS code. These are considered public charities and all donations to them are tax exempt. Charitynavigator.com and charitablechoices.org provide ratings for thousands of charities—all of which have been granted this status—and give information on how much of the money they receive actually goes toward their mission (versus administrative, publicity, or other costs). Also, don't forget to check and see if your employer offers a matching program. Many large corporations will match your donations to specific charities dollar-for-dollar. If money is tight, why not volunteer your time instead? Most organizations could use extra manpower as well as money.

money back, but your donation can help to lower your taxes. Clothing donations are tax deductible. Just don't forget to document your donations carefully. Ask for a receipt from the charity estimating the monetary value of your donation.

3. **Evaluate the essentials:** There are certain items that *every* woman needs in her closet, no matter where you live. These include:
   - a little black dress (simple and stylish)
   - a classic button-up white shirt
   - a pair of good jeans
   - a rainproof coat (trench coats never go out of style)
   - a pair of dress pants (black is best)
   - a suit (either pants or a skirt and a matching blazer)
   - a basic everyday bag (in a neutral color)
   - a classic sweater (a V-neck, scoop neck, or cardigan that you can throw over your shirt when the temperature dips)
   - a pair of black pumps
   - a pair of boots (flat or heeled, dressy or casual, depending on your lifestyle)

   If you're missing any of these, put them at the top of your shopping list.

4. **Build around the basics:** Spend your money first on the essential building blocks of your wardrobe, like those listed above. These items should last for years, so it's worth spending a bit more on them. In addition to the fashion fundamentals, there may be some pieces that you decide to buy or replace each season or every few seasons—from a winter coat (unless you live someplace warm) to a pair of boots to a swimsuit. As you shop to expand your inventory, think about additions that will pair well with your essential items (a top to wear under the suit, for example, or a wrap to wear over your black dress).

5. **Mix & match:** Each new item of clothing or accessory that you purchase should enhance your existing wardrobe. Before you buy

anything new, ask yourself how many different outfits you could make by combining this new item with the clothes that are currently in your closet. Unless you're buying something for a special occasion, like a wedding, you should be able to come up with at least four fabulous outfit combinations you could put together immediately after buying this item.

6. **Know what's trendy versus timeless:** Once you've got lots of basic items that you can mix and match in your closet and hold on to for a while, you can start adding flair: fun clothes, shoes, and accessories that look cool now but may be past their prime by next year. Set aside a little money to spend on those trendier items that can freshen up your closet for the season. There's nothing wrong with following fads. Just remember that they don't last long; that's why they're called fads. So spend accordingly.

7. **Don't knock knockoffs:** Within weeks of the major fashion shows, stores like H&M, T.J. Maxx, Target, or Zara are already selling copies of the latest designer trends for discount prices. Since these styles probably won't last more than a season or two anyway, it's smarter to spend less on them and save more for those classic pieces that you can keep in your closet for years. These stores do a great job of capturing the look of the moment for less. They're also great places to pick up simple T-shirts and trousers and accessories to mix and match with your better-quality basics.

8. **Get luxury for less:** You don't need to drop a lot of money to own designer brands. Look for discounted merchandise at sample sales or used on eBay. Or see if your favorite designer is offering a less expensive line. Target and H&M have both paired with well-known designers, from Proenza Schouler and Isaac Mizrahi to Karl Lagerfeld and Stella McCartney. Many upscale retailers also have discount outlets (think Saks Fifth Avenue's Off 5th) that are often clustered together in outlet shopping centers. You can get some great bargains on luxury brands.

9. **Share & swap:** If you're sick of your clothes, or you want a new look for a special occasion but don't want to spend a lot, ask your similar-sized friends if you can "shop" in their closets. Or organize a swap. Each person brings a few good items of clothing that they're ready to replace, and then you swap items with one another. Your friends often have a different sense of style, so it's fun to try on the clothes that they brought. You might not have picked them out yourself in a store, but they may look great on you. Plus, this way you know your clothes are in good hands (should you ever decide you miss them), and you've got new clothes to spruce up your style without spending a cent. Sharing clothes with your friends is also an easy way to give your wardrobe a boost without spending money. We do it all the time. In just one year, we saved about $5,000 by swapping outfits instead of shopping for new clothes for dates, weddings, and work functions.

10. **Avoid deadline or emotional shopping:** If you wait until the night before a big trip to buy last-minute outfits, you're sure to overspend. You've likely convinced yourself you need certain items, and as the clock ticks, you'll become more desperate to have them regardless of the cost. Same goes for dates, weddings, or any special occasion. If you're short on time, consider borrowing a few items from a friend instead. Or wear something you already have in your closet but buy a new wrap or a necklace to update it. Always have a backup plan so you don't get stuck spending too much.

    Emotional shopping is just as dangerous. How many times have you "treated" yourself to a shopping trip to try to lift your spirits? Though you may feel some elation right after you buy a new outfit, the trip often ends up having the opposite effect once you realize how much money you spent. Plus, you may find when you get home that the great new shirt goes with nothing in your closet. But you weren't thinking about that when you bought it—in fact, you weren't thinking at all. You were fueled by pure emotion. When you have moments like these, it's time to enlist the help of your friends and money-group members. That's why we've devised a system we call:

In Case of (a Spending) Emergency, Call . . .

Remember those names you wrote down in Chapter One—three people to whom you'd feel comfortable confiding your financial problems? These are friends and family you know will support you in achieving your financial goals and sticking to your spending plan. Ask if you can make them your "In Case of (a Spending) Emergency" buddies too. During those moments of weakness when you're tempted to buy something you know you probably shouldn't, you can call one of them and they'll remind you why you'd *rather* save your money for something else.

Rip out a couple of pages from your notebook. On each page, list your contacts' names and telephone numbers. Then, on the other side of each piece of paper, list the financial goals you came up with in Chapter Three. (You can also download a card from our website.) You can keep one page posted on your mirror or fridge and carry the other one in your wallet, to keep yourself motivated when you're tempted to stray from your budget or to pull out the plastic. Before you make any purchase, ask yourself if it's more important than getting to your financial goal that much faster. Just by framing each spending decision that way, you will find that sticking to your spending plan becomes easier. And as you get used to finding small ways to save money every day, you may decide you want to redo your spending plan so that you're saving more for your larger goals or paying off your debt even faster. In the next chapter, we'll walk you through six steps to get you back in the black as quickly and painlessly as possible.

Smart Cookie Summary

Discussion Questions:

1. How often do you use cash and why?
2. Have you ever gotten rid of a perfectly functioning item because you worried it was outdated? Why?
3. What expenses do you think you could cut without noticing much difference in your daily life?
4. What suggestions do you have to save money in other areas of your life, like shopping or going out?
5. How much do you want to set aside for fun money? What are some ways you would spend it?

Smart Steps:

1. Create a spending plan that's built around your financial goals.
2. Take the quiz to see what kind of spender you are. List three steps you can take to avoid overspending.
3. Over the next week, or before the next meeting if you're in a group, try out one of the suggestions for saving money that are listed in this chapter, or come up with one of your own.
4. Set aside a time when you will clean out your closet and dump, donate, or sell the clothes and accessories you decide not to keep. If you don't have time now, take on a smaller project. Clean out a drawer or go through your books and recycle or sell those you no longer want.
5. Fill out your In Case of (a Spending) Emergency card, and make sure that those you've listed understand their important roles.

chapter 5

Deflate Your Debt

Six Simple Steps to Get You Back in the Black

There's a good chance you're carrying around some kind of debt, whether it's a revolving line of credit at your bank, a credit card (or two or three), or a loan you took out to cover the costs of college or a new car. Most Americans are. Even if you're able to manage the minimum monthly payments with ease, it may feel like you'll never be able to start making any real money until that debt is fully paid off. The good news is: You can. Yes, it's important that you pay off any balances you owe, particularly if they come with a high interest rate. But carrying debt shouldn't keep you from accumulating wealth. And, as we'll explain later in this chapter, sometimes it makes more sense financially to invest extra earnings into a stock fund or a money-market account than to use it to pay off a debt faster. We'll also help you prioritize your payments. But before we do that, it's important to distinguish between the different types of debts you may have.

The Good, the Bad, and the Downright Dangerous

THE GOOD:

It's best to owe nothing, of course, but not all debt is "bad." Taking on certain types of debt may actually help you make more money in the long run. Taking out a mortgage to buy a home, for example, can more than pay for itself if the home goes up in value—and, over the long term, you can expect it to do so. Yes, the real estate market cooled down considerably in 2008, with home prices falling in most parts of the country, but, historically, real estate values go up over the long run. Four of us have purchased homes, and all of them have appreciated in value since we bought them a few years ago. We'll go into more detail on investing in real estate in Chapter Eight.

Getting a government loan to attend college or graduate school may also be worth the investment if you know the degree will help increase your income potential. Robyn literally doubled her earnings by attaining a master's degree in social work. And there's little question that having a master's degree in business administration or a medical or law degree will help you obtain a high-paying job. Still, it's smart to see if you can finance at least some of the costs of tuition yourself or if you're eligible for grants or scholarships that don't require repayment.

The federal Pell Grant program, for example, provides need-based grants to very low-income undergraduate and some postgraduate students that may be used at any of about 5,400 participating U.S. schools. Plus, there are literally tens of thousands of scholarships out there, many of which are not even based on financial need. There are a myriad of unusual scholarships for applicants with certain attributes—like being left-handed, a twin, or extremely tall—or for those who either enter a contest (like the National Make It Yourself with Wool competition, which awards $2,000 and $1,000 scholarships for knitting winning wool garments) or agree to pursue an unusual field of study (like the American Association of Candy Technologists' annual $5,000 scholarship for college students with an interest in "confectionary technology"). There are also several scholarships available for "mature" students—those who have chosen to pursue a college or graduate degree in their mid-20s, 30s, or beyond. The Newcombe Scholarship for Mature Women, for example, has given out more than $12 million to older students since it was created in 1981 (check out www.new combefoundation.org for more information). In the 2006–2007 school year, the average recipient was 37 years old. It's never too late to go back to school. Yes, many of the scholarships we mentioned are a little out of the ordinary. But our point is: You'd be surprised by the amount of aid available out there, if you're willing to look for it. If you're thinking about pursuing a degree, a good place to start your search is one of these sites: finaid.org, collegeboard.com, and scholarships.com. They are great, free sources for scholarship information.

Don't forget that many companies also offer full or partial tuition coverage for employees. Andrea used the $2,000 per year her former employer offered to take four night classes in marketing and other related topics and to pay for textbooks too. Many employers offer additional assistance for those who pursue an advanced degree while working, if you can demonstrate how the degree will improve your skills and performance at work. Of course, the flip side is that your employer may require you to remain at the company for a set period of time after you've obtained your degree. So be careful if you're pursuing an additional degree to get a better-paying job someplace else.

If you don't have time to commute to a class after work, or you want more flexibility, many universities now offer online degrees. They can also be less expensive, since the university saves money by not using classroom space and supplies—and think of the money you'll save on gas and parking (not to mention the time you'll save by not commuting).

Taking out a loan to start your own business is another type of debt that can pay off in the long run. Starting a business is risky, though; more businesses fail than thrive. It's smart to have some start-up money of your own or at least a cushion to help you through the rough times. It may make sense to turn first to friends and family who believe in you and your business for financial help. They're likely to charge you less interest and allow a longer payoff period. They can also help absorb some of the risk, if you offer them a piece of the business rather than a specific repayment amount for their loan. Still, make sure to do your homework before you approach *anyone* for start-up money. You should have a solid business plan ready to present to any potential investors. A good resource is the U.S. Small Business Administration (sba.gov). This government agency does not give out grants to start or expand small businesses, but it does offer a wide variety of loan programs and resources. The website not only provides step-by-step instructions on how to write a business plan, but it has links to sample business plans for start-ups ranging from a scrapbooking store to a yoga center.

The Small Business Administration also provides free counseling and training through partnerships with groups like the SCORE Association (Service Corps of Retired Executives), the Office of Small Business Development Centers, and the Women's Business Centers (a network of about 100 centers nationwide that provide help for women starting or expanding their own businesses). There are also several women's groups like Count Me In (countmein.org), Ladies Who Launch (ladieswholaunch.com), and the Forum for Women Entrepreneurs and Executives (fwe.org), which offer workshops and networking events, though there's usually a charge to join or attend. You can also seek out the advice of someone you trust who's started a successful business. (We are huge advocates of seeking the advice and support of mentors. Each of us has one.) Have your business plan evaluated and make adjustments to it—and to your expectations—*before* you quit your day job or take out a hefty loan.

THE BAD:

While a mortgage is generally a "good" source of debt, that doesn't mean that taking out adjustable second mortgages or home-equity loans is a good idea.

Borrowing against your home with the assumption that interest rates will stay low and your home's value will continue to increase can be dangerous. You've probably seen the commercials, showing happy homeowners who took out home-equity loans to pay off their credit-card debt or to cover their child's college education. There's nothing wrong with tapping into your home equity in certain situations. If your home has appreciated in value and you plan to use the money you borrow to pay off all your high-interest credit-card debt, for example, taking out a home-equity loan at a low rate can be the right move. (This is essentially what Andrea did.) But if you don't have a fixed rate and interest rates climb, as they did in 2006 and 2007, your monthly payments will too—as many homeowners learned the hard way. If the value of your home doesn't increase very much, or actually declines, in the meantime (a real risk in the 2008 housing market), you could actually *lose* money on your investment. Worse, if you're unable to keep up with the mortgage and home-equity loan payments, you could lose your house. Foreclosure filings were up 75 percent in 2007 from the year before, with nearly 1.3 million properties—or about one in every 100 U.S. households—in some state of foreclosure, according to RealtyTrac, which markets foreclosed properties. Those are extremely scary statistics.

Having your car repossessed isn't nearly as scary as losing your home. But it's a major embarrassment, not to mention a major inconvenience. According to recent reports, however, it's happening to a growing number of Americans this year, for the same reason that so many homes are going into foreclosure. A few years ago—when interest rates were low, getting a loan was relatively easy, and the economy was doing well—consumers were more willing to stretch themselves to get a more expensive car. Now that the economy has slowed down, and the interest rates on some loans have increased, many of these car owners are struggling to cover their monthly payments, not to mention the gas they need to get around (with fuel $4 or more a gallon in mid-2008). The result? The number of cars and trucks being repossessed this year is expected to climb to 1.6 million—a ten percent increase from last year and the highest number in at least a decade, according to an article in *USA Today*.

Of course, we realize that unless you live in a city with good public transportation, you're probably going to need a car to get around. And if you don't have enough money to buy a car outright and don't want to lease one, you'll need to finance it. But car loans fall into the "bad" debt category because you're likely to pay a lot more for one, including the interest, than you'll ever get from reselling the car, and—as we mentioned above—if you can't keep up with your car payments, you can lose your car. Buying a car is an investment only in the sense that you are investing in reliable transportation to get you to work and back so you can earn a paycheck. Your car starts losing value the second you drive it off the lot. So, in the traditional sense, it's a bad investment. Use a loan to buy a new car from a dealership and you may still be paying off your loan long after the car has been resold or towed away to a junkyard. Your best bet? Unless you're wealthy enough to pay for the car in cash, we recommend you buy a used model instead and scout out classified ads or online car sales to find the best deal. You can often buy a used car that's just two to four years old at a savings of 25 to 50 percent less than what it would cost new, according to *Road & Travel* magazine. Check *Consumer Reports* (consumerreports.org) or Kelley Blue Book (kbb.com) for more ratings and research on specific models and the best resale values. If you do decide to buy a new car, it's best to wait until the end of the year when the upcoming year's models start coming in and dealerships are trying to clear out inventory to make room for them. Then it will be easier to ask for a lower price on the current models.

If you can pay cash, most sellers are also likely to accept a lower price for a used car. For the best deal, try buying directly from the car owner, through classified ads or craigslist.org. Just make sure to have a trusted mechanic look it over before you hand over your money. If you need to finance part of the sale, shop around for a loan—through credit unions, banks, or the automakers' financing arms (like GMAC)—*before* you shop for the car. That way you can make sure to get the best interest rate, and you'll get an idea of how much money you can reasonably afford to borrow so you'll know what price range to stick with when you look for a car.

Financing a car is only good in the sense that you actually have something to show for the money you've borrowed. If you're in a bind, you can sell your car and use the money you make to pay off a good chunk of the amount you borrowed, though chances are you won't make enough to pay off the loan entirely, unless you only relied on financing to cover a small amount of the initial cost of the car. The best advice is to use cash to pay for the car and skip the financing. If you're married, consider sharing a car with your spouse. Or, if you live in a major city with good public transportation, put off the purchase altogether and use the transit system to get around. In cities with a sophisticated, reliable public system like New York, Boston, or San Francisco, having a car may actually be more of a burden than hopping on the bus or subway—certainly from a financial standpoint. You could easily pay $400 or more per month just to park your car in a Manhattan garage, for example (almost as much as some people pay for rent in other parts of the country!), while a monthly unlimited-use MetroCard costs $81. If you need a car for a specific event—to visit relatives for the holidays, for example—you can rent one for a few days or take advantage of a car-share program (which we describe below). Remember to reserve a car well in advance of any major holiday.

As part of her plan to save money for a new home and for her upcoming wedding, Katie decided to get rid of her car and use the bus, take a cab, or carpool with friends or her then-fiancé instead. It was a tough adjustment at first. But within 18 months, she'd already saved more than $6,000 in parking charges, insurance, gas, oil changes, and estimated repairs! And she found it was a lot easier to use public transport and work out a schedule with her fiancé than she'd imagined. Sandra also decided she didn't need her own car. Instead, she signed up with a car-sharing service called Zipcar (www.zipcar.com). Joining the service, which has cars in more than 20 major metropolitan areas, requires a onetime application fee and often a monthly prepay (that goes toward the use of the car) and additional payments for rentals that exceed the prepaid amount. That's not hard to do—daily rates hovered around $60, hourly rates around $9, in early 2008. But for those like Sandra, smart bite

TRIM TRANSPORTATION COSTS: If you do have a car and live in New York, Boston, Washington, D.C., or Philadelphia, check out bestparking.com for the best daily and monthly garage rates (the site only offered information on those four cities as of April 2008, but plans to add more). Another way to cut costs is by carpooling or sharing your car and expenses with other coworkers or commuters in your area. Founded in 1999, eRideShare.com is one of the largest car-pool/ride-sharing websites serving the United States and Canada, with more than 15,000 commuter, travel, and local ride-share listings. Just plug in your zip code to find listings in your area. If you're in a major city, you can save money on cab fare by visiting Rideamigos.com, which lets you link up with others in your neighborhood who are looking for a cab to popular locations like the area airports or sports stadiums or who have a similar daily commuting route. As of the fall of 2007, it was operating in New York, San Francisco, Los Angeles, and Chicago. Members just create an account, enter their ride criteria, and a list of matching posts will appear.

who mostly rely on other kinds of transportation—like her roommate or the bus—it can be worth it. (Another service, FlexCar, merged with Zipcar in the fall of 2007.)

THE DOWNRIGHT DANGEROUS:

Credit cards, as you've probably guessed, represent the worst kind of debt. That's not just because you are likely to pay higher interest rates on a credit-card balance than you would for a mortgage or school loan but because carrying a credit-card balance is an indication that you're over-spending on a regular basis. A credit card lets you pretend you can afford a lifestyle that's actually beyond your means—for a little while, anyway—instead of taking action to ensure you *can* actually afford the life you want. It's a double whammy. Not only can you end up paying as much as 30 per-cent more for your purchase when you use a card than you would have if you'd used cash, but you get into the practice of just pulling out plastic and paying for it later (and, boy, will you pay!) rather than saving up money for something you want. With credit cards, you end up paying so much for your past behavior that it's difficult to prepare for the future you want.

If you charge just $2,500 on a credit card with a 12 percent annual interest rate and send in minimum monthly payments that cover 2 percent of the balance, it could take you more than 19 years to get rid of your debt and you'll end up paying more than $2,200 in interest alone—almost as much as you borrowed in the first place!

Ever wonder how your interest-rate payment is calculated each month? Here's how it breaks down: Essentially, your bank looks at what you owe on your card every day. So let's say you have a balance of $4,000. The bank would multiply that number by your interest-rate percentage. If you have a card with a 19 percent annual percentage rate (or APR), for example, you'd multiply 4,000 by .19 to get $760. Then that number is divided by 365 (for the number of days in the year). That means, *each* day you're being charged $2.08. It's as if your credit-card company is reaching into your wallet every day and taking out two dollars! Not only that, but the interest adds up between payments, so what you're charged each month is actually based on your "average daily balance." That means your balance can go above $4,000 as interest is added, and then you're charged interest on the interest! That's why cutting your interest rate just a little, or paying off your balance even one month sooner, can make a big differ-ence. Keep in mind that the interest you're charged can also bump you over your credit limit. That's what happened to Andrea. She'd stopped just short of maxing out a card, but then the interest her card issuer charged her pushed her balance over the limit. She had to pay an additional $20 fee, plus the interest and enough to make sure she didn't exceed her limit again.

That is getting more challenging for many cardholders. If you're a regular credit-card user, you are getting hit particularly hard these days because issuers are allowed to jack up interest rates seemingly arbitrarily and to charge additional fees.

What We've Learned—and You Should Know—about Credit Cards

Did you know that if you make a late payment on a car loan—even if it's just a few hours overdue—the interest you pay on *all* your credit-card balances could conceivably double? One-third of all U.S. credit-card holders are now paying interest rates of 20 percent or more. You can bet that some, if not all, of them didn't start out paying that much. Not only that, but late fees themselves are more costly than they used to be. According to CardWeb.com, Inc., credit-card late fees have nearly tripled since 1995, from an average of about $13 to nearly $34 in 2005! That same year, more than one-third of all active credit-card accounts in the country were assessed a late fee at least once, according to a New York State Consumer Protection Board report.

The so-called "Universal Default" provision, which allows card issuers to increase the interest rate they're charging on a particular card to the default rate (which can be 29.99 percent or more!) when cardholders are late with other payments or their credit score declines, is only one of several practices that can result in your paying much more than you expected on the credit you borrowed. Others, as of spring 2008, include:

- Double-cycle billing: This allows the card issuer to charge interest on debt that has been repaid, if the cardholder pays only part of the balance by the due date. So let's say you charge a $100 dress on your card on October 1, and your bill is sent out November 5 and due November 20. You submit a payment of $60, which is credited on November 18. That leaves a $40 balance at the end of the period. But the card issuer can charge you interest on the entire balance of $100 for that period of October 1 to November 18, according to the American Bankers Association. In 2006, about one-third of card issuers used this practice, according to a report by the Government Accountability Office, though some have since stopped.

- Penalty rates: These are "penalty" increases in the actual annual percentage rate for a credit card, triggered when you make a late monthly payment, for example, or you exceed your credit limit (even if it's the assessment of a card fee that pushes you over the limit). The APR can then jump as high as 30 or even 40 percent! And it may be applied not only to new purchases but to your existing balance.

- Late-payment triggers: Credit-card issuers used to be more forgiving, especially if your due date fell on a holiday or weekend. But now, if the payment is not *posted* to the account by the due date, it will be considered late. That means, even if you sent the payment in a week early, but it didn't post to your account until the day after it was due, you'll be assessed a late fee—and, worse, it could allow other credit-card issuers to assess penalties or default rates too.

- Unilateral change-in-terms: This allows credit-card issuers to change *any* term of the contract with the cardholder with only a 15-day notice, according to the Truth in Lending Act. So make sure to read the fine print of any notice you get from your card issuer immediately so you can review the new terms and have the chance to ask your issuer to opt out before the changes take effect.

- Shorter turnaround times: If it seems like your bill is arriving closer to the due date than it used to, you're probably not imagining it. Consumer advocates found that some credit-card companies are sending their monthly statements out later in the month, giving their customers less time to make their payments before the due date. That may also prompt more to pay online or by phone, which can result in additional fees. Generally, fees are assessed only for express payments, which are made on the due date, but sometimes card issuers simply charge a fee to use the service at all. So check first.

- Payment allocation: This allows issuers to apply your monthly payments first to the portion of your debt subject to the lowest interest rate. For example, if you're paying 18 percent on purchases you made, but just 1.99 percent on a balance you transferred from another credit card, your monthly payments will go first to pay the lower interest balance, while the 18 percent interest continues to accrue on your other balance.

Congress has been considering credit-card legislation that could help cardholders by protecting against arbitrary interest-rate increases, preventing card issuers from charging excessive fees, and providing more transparency in credit-card statements. And the Federal Reserve Board has proposed similar regulations. But neither regulations nor legislation had passed by the spring of 2008 and, even if they are eventually adopted, credit-card companies may find other means of increasing the amount you pay. Some banks are cutting back on the most punitive practices. But watch out for anything unusual on your monthly statements.

One tactic card issuers use is discontinuing a particular card and automatically switching its users to a new card, often with a higher interest rate. This happened to one of us. If this happens to you, you'll get written notification—and don't be fooled if the letter starts with a congratulatory message to its "valued" customer or gushes about the new card's special features. Read the fine print! If the card carries a higher interest rate, call the issuer immediately and ask to be switched to a different card that has the same (or lower—why not?) interest rate as the one that was discontinued.

Also, if you take advantage of a balance transfer offer, keep a close eye on the interest rate listed in each monthly statement. Did you know that card issuers can increase even the special promotional rate you signed up for?

A CAUTIONARY TALE
(Angela)

I was thrilled to be able to transfer my balance on a credit card with an annual interest rate of 11.5 percent to one with an annual interest rate of less than 2 percent. Under the promotion, I would have this special rate for just six months. So I created a payment plan that would allow me to pay off the entire credit-card balance over the course of those six months. I set aside a specific amount each month for my credit card, but if I came into additional money it went straight to pay down that balance.

Two months into the offer, I received a statement and noticed that my interest rate was now listed at 3.97 percent. Yes, this was still a low rate, but it wasn't the one that I had been promised. I couldn't believe that the card issuer had increased my interest without even notifying me. (Or if it did, it was buried deep within the fine print.) I immediately called up the credit-card company. The representative I spoke with tried to convince me that they had changed the rate for my benefit because they planned to keep the higher interest rate in place for as long as I needed to pay off the balance. But I didn't plan on having a balance after the six-month promotional time. After some back and forth, the company finally agreed to reduce my interest rate to the original promotional rate. Prior to joining the money group I had never looked at my credit-card bills or my interest rate. I would have blindly paid the extra money in interest charges without even realizing it. Not anymore!

We're not saying that you should cut up all your credit cards and never apply for another. Using credit cards responsibly can help to build your credit history and credit rating. But we recommend that you not use a credit card unless you can pay off your balance each month.

Ultimately, we want you to improve your credit score and get rid of as much debt as possible—whether it's "good" or "bad." Based on our experience and research, we've come up with six simple steps to get you on your way. Obviously, if you have no debt, you can skip right to the end of this chapter, and kudos to you! But for the rest of you, read on.

Getting Back in the Black

Step One:

TALLY UP YOUR TOTALS

For this exercise, you'll need to collect your most recent mortgage, credit-card, bank, and car-loan statements. You can photocopy the work sheet on the following page, or download one from our site. On it, you'll list: the total unpaid balance on each debt, the interest you're paying, the minimum monthly payment, and how long you've had each loan or credit-card balance. Want a reality check? Use the online calculator at bankrate.com (www.bankrate.com/brm/calc/creditcardpay.asp) or fool.com to analyze how long it will take you to repay that debt if you continue to make the same payments. We'll bet it's longer than you figured. But don't worry. We're going to help you speed up your repayment plan.

Step Two:

PRIORITIZE YOUR PAYMENTS

Now, in your notebook or on the back of the work sheet, list your outstanding balances in order of highest interest rate to lowest interest rate. This will help

	LENDER NAME	BALANCE	INTEREST RATE	MINIMUM PAYMENT	HOW LONG YOU'VE HAD IT
Credit Card #1					
Credit Card #2					
Credit Card #3					
Credit Card #4					
Mortgage					
Car Loan					
Student Loans					
Line of Credit					
Other					
Other					
Other					

you decide which to pay off first. In some cases, if the interest rates are close but one balance is significantly lower than another, it's worth paying that off first for the satisfaction of having one less monthly payment that you can now use toward another debt. But, as a general rule, it's best to pay off the balance with the highest interest rate first. Paying a high-interest balance off even a few months sooner can save you $100 or more in interest charges. That can go toward paying your next balance off even faster (assuming you have another one).

This list will change as you pay off your debts and lower your interest rates, which leads us to . . .

Step Three:

BE A CARD SHARK

We urge you to try to lower the interest you are paying on every credit-card, car, or bank loan. There's a good chance that you can decrease the amount of interest you're paying on your balance, especially if you have a good payment history (no late or missed payments, for example) and have held this card for a long period of time (say, five years). But you can be darn sure that your bank isn't going to offer it to you. You'll have to ask for it, politely but persistently. One effective way is to use balance transfer offers you've received from other banks as leverage. Your card issuer doesn't want to lose your business if they can help it, and they are often willing to lower your interest rate to keep your money.

Don't give up easily. You will often need to ask for a supervisor to authorize a lower rate or even ask about switching your balance to another card offered by the same bank that has a lower rate but fewer bells and whistles. Make it clear to the supervisor that you don't need points, "rewards," or other features; you just want a plain vanilla card that comes with the lowest interest rate available. (After all, you don't plan to actually use this card anymore for purchases—you just want to pay off the balance.)

HOW WE DID IT
Earning Real Rewards
(Sandra)

I called to lower the interest rate I was being charged on my credit-card balance a few months after I joined the money group. I was using a Visa card that promised shopping "rewards" after I'd charged a specific amount—like discounts on specific purchases—but I was being charged an interest rate of 19.5 percent on the $2,000 balance I was carrying. When I called the credit-card company and asked to lower my interest rate, I was firm and told the representative that I was prepared to take my business elsewhere if she couldn't offer me a lower rate. After some discussion, I was informed that the company would gladly lower my interest rate to 11.5 percent but only if I would change my card to a "no rewards" card. After thinking it over, I agreed to change my card. I hoped the difference in interest rates would be worth it. When I got off the phone, I examined my statements to be sure. I realized that the rewards I was earning on the original card added up to a savings of about $50 every six months in shopping or gas money. But I was paying $120 in interest during the same time period! Even just by cutting the rate by eight percent, it clearly made sense to go with the card that offered no frills but a lower interest rate. Saving the money each month in interest charges was the real reward.

If you are unable to convince your bank to match a transfer offer, transfer the balance. But make sure to check for hidden fees and limited-time offers. Some banks offer low balance-transfer rates for a limited period—say, six months to a year—before the interest on that balance reverts back to a higher rate, which can be more than the rate you were paying on the other card! So be sure that you'll either be able to pay off the entire balance within the limited offer period or that the interest rate it bumps up to is lower than what you're paying now to justify moving the balance over. Make sure to ask the representative exactly what the rate will be after the set period and whether it is fixed or variable. See if you can get that in writing. You don't want to be surprised in six months when the variable rate has climbed past 19 percent because federal benchmark rates have increased in the interim. Make sure to ask the bank that sends you the balance offer what the lifetime balance offer would be, if there is one available. It may be two or three points higher but still less than what you're paying now. And if you know you'll need more than six months to pay if off, it may be worth it to secure a lifetime fixed-interest rate on the balance you transferred. Finally, be sure to ask if the transfer fees can be waived or, if not, how much the transfer will cost you. You'll likely be charged a percentage of the amount you're transferring—typically about three percent, up to a maximum of $75. So make sure it's worth transferring the money. Do the calculations to be sure that you'll save at least as much with the lower interest rate as it will cost you to transfer the balance. If you have a big balance and don't think you'll be able to pay it off for several months, the fee is usually worth it. But if you owe $2,500 and will pay a $75 fee (three percent), it might make sense not to transfer the balance and just make sure that paying it off becomes your priority.

Step Four:

CONSIDER CONSOLIDATION

You may be able to save money on interest by consolidating your loans. But be sure that the interest rate is low enough to justify the transfer. Beware consolidators who try to lure you with the promise of long-term pay periods or who are not up front about the interest and fees you'll be paying. Long-term pay periods often mean you're paying a lot more interest. And if you're having trouble getting information up front on the interest you'll pay, chances are it's not a good rate.

There are other ways of paying off your credit-card debt if you own your home, particularly if it goes up in value. Andrea, for example, had improved her credit enough and built up so much equity in her condo by 2007—about $150,000—that she was able to pay off her remaining credit line and credit-card debt. Her bank gave her a loan to pay off the debt and then tacked it onto her mortgage, keeping the monthly payments the same but extending her mortgage repayment period by two years. She made sure that her mortgage terms would allow her to make extra payments without being penalized, though, and she voluntarily pays more than she needs to on her monthly mortgage payments since she no longer has to make credit-card payments. Not only did she save thousands in credit-card interest payments, but she now has no credit-card debt and just one manageable monthly payment. Plus, she's been able to bank the money she used to put toward her credit line and Visa payments, so she's actually *earning* interest on it rather than paying interest. And she plans to pay off her mortgage before it winds down to the last two years, so she won't have to pay that additional interest either.

Step Five:

FIX YOUR FICO

Missing or falling behind on credit-card payments is NOT Smart Cookie approved—and it's a pretty obvious no-no if you're trying to be financially responsible and avoid unnecessary fees and interest hikes. But there are several other mistakes you may unwittingly make that can cause long-term damage to your FICO scores—the credit scores most lenders use to determine your credit risk—and to your credit report, without your even realizing it. Did you know, for example, that if you enroll in a credit-counseling or debt-management plan, it can be noted on your credit report for seven years? Of course, that won't affect your credit rating as much as defaulting, or being severely delinquent, on the debt you owe. But it does tell creditors that you were unable to stay on top of your debts on your own.

If you're in way over your head and are falling behind on even your minimum monthly payments, a credit-counseling agency can help to renegotiate your interest rates and minimum payments and set up a payment plan so you can avoid bankruptcy or defaulting on your debt. But be wary of agencies that charge big fees or make big promises. A slew of debt-management companies have sprung up in the wake of the rapid rise in consumer debt. Most of the worst offenders have been put out of business, but it's still smart to watch out for those that charge fees up front or ask for large monthly fees to service your account. In general, you should not expect to pay more than $75 in setup fees. Before you sign up with a credit-counseling agency, check with the Better Business Bureau in your area to see if any complaints have been lodged against it. Look for accredited, licensed organizations with certified credit counselors. The National Foundation for Credit Counselors (nfcc.org) or the Association of Independent Consumer Credit Counseling Agencies (AICCCA.org), or Consolidated Credit Counseling Services, Inc., (consolidatedcredit.org) can provide aid over the phone, or give you the names of member credit-counseling agencies in your area; the AICCCA also has a toll-free referral line: 1-800-450-1794. Keep in mind that your creditors should be credited with 100 percent of the amount you pay through a credit-counseling agency (in other words—make sure the entire debt payment you send to the agency is going toward your balance). And, remember, while a credit counselor can help to renegotiate your monthly payments, the interest you're paying, and sometimes even the amount you must repay to avoid defaulting on your debt, the repayment plan may be noted on your credit report for years to come. You may also be in trouble if the agency you work with sends in one of your payments late. Before you enlist the help of an outside agency, try calling your creditors directly to explain your financial situation and see if you can work out a payment plan that you're able to afford. If that doesn't work, a credit counselor may be able to negotiate more successfully for lower rates. But be sure to ask what steps you can take to minimize any long-term damage to your credit.

EXTRA CREDIT

Most of you probably aren't in need of a credit counselor's intervention. But do you know how credit worthy you are? Your FICO credit scores can range from about 300 to 850 and are calculated by the Fair Isaac Corporation (named after founders Bill Fair and Earl Isaac), based on information from each of the three major credit-reporting bureaus: Equifax, Experian, and TransUnion. That's why you may have a slightly different score depending on the agency through which you get your score. Why does the number matter so much? The higher the score, the lower the risk you are considered to be to a creditor—and the less interest you'll pay. Fair Isaac uses a proprietary formula. But we'll let you in on some of the factors it uses to crunch the numbers and how much weight is given to each. Generally, here's how your FICO scores break down:

- 35 percent = payment history
- 30 percent = amounts owed on each account
- 15 percent = length of credit (how long you've had the accounts)
- 10 percent = new credit (new accounts opened or inquiries made for more credit)
- 10 percent = types of credit in use (e.g., credit card, department store, mortgage, or school loans)

There are simple ways to improve your score in each category:

PAYMENT HISTORY
- Pay your monthly payments on time.
- If you are having trouble keeping up with payments, notify your lender that you need to work out an arrangement and then get current on any past-due accounts as soon as possible.

AMOUNTS OWED
- Keep low balances relative to your credit limit: Keeping your total balance at 35 percent or less than your total credit available is good. (Though, of course, a zero balance is best!)
- The level of revolving debt (like credit cards) is one of the most important factors in determining your FICO score. The credit agencies look at your balances both in relation to your total available credit and to your individual revolving accounts. Opening new accounts just to make your outstanding balances look smaller in relation to your total credit capacity won't help; in fact, it could actually hurt if you rack up more debt

on those accounts. Opening too many new lines of credit, even if you don't use them, could also lower your FICO score. (Agencies get suspicious when you apply for an excessive amount of credit in a particular period.)

LENGTH OF CREDIT

- Consider keeping old accounts open if you've been a good borrower (even if you are transferring the balance to a different card). Instead of improving your credit, as you'd think it would, closing an account actually erases your good payment history from your report (assuming you had a good history and didn't miss or fall behind on any payments). So erasing the card can actually hurt your credit history, which is a critical factor in determining your score. It's better to cut up the card but leave the account alone.

NEW-CREDIT CATEGORY

- When shopping for new credit, keep the search to a short time frame—aim for 14 days or less. You can hurt your score if there are a number of credit inquiries over time for applications like credit cards, auto loans, department-store credit cards, etc., that *you* have initiated. FICO scores distinguish between a search for a single loan and a search for several new sources of credit in part by the length of time over which your inquiries occur. (Note: If a card issuer inquires about your report without your knowledge, it should not affect your score.)
- If you've got a spotty credit history, you can improve your credit score by opening a new credit card with a low limit (if you're able to qualify for one) and managing it responsibly—by paying off the balance each month, for example. Then you'll avoid paying interest too.

smart SC bite

GET A FREE COPY OF YOUR CREDIT REPORT: Requesting a copy of your credit report or score for personal use does NOT affect your credit score, no matter how many requests you make, as long as you order it directly from a credit-reporting agency or through an organization that's authorized to provide reports to consumers (versus a credit card offer that promises to give you a free credit report too). In fact, you're entitled to one free copy of your credit report each year from each of the three major credit bureaus, though they're not required to provide your score. Be aware that only one website is authorized to fill orders for the free annual credit report: www.annualcreditreport.com. There are several others that sound similar. Many promise "free" credit scores and reports (like freecreditreport.com or freecredit reportasap.com) but require you to enroll in a "free" trial membership in one of their programs in order to see it. If you don't cancel your membership within 30 days, you may be billed as much as $29.95 each month until you do so. You can purchase your score and monitoring services for less from one of the three credit bureaus themselves: Equifax (equifax.com), Experian (experian .com), or TransUnion (transunion.com).

TYPES OF CREDIT
- Having so-called "installment" debt (where you pay fixed monthly installments to eliminate the debt, like a mortgage) is considered better than having "revolving" debt, like credit-card balances.
- Having certain finance-company debts (like using retailer financing to

buy furniture or other big-ticket items) may also be less desirable than having a mortgage or other "installment" debts.

Before she joined the Smart Cookies, Robyn says she fell behind on credit-card payments on more than one occasion. She often sent off payments toward her credit-card balances whenever she had a little extra money, with no regard to due dates. Not surprisingly, her credit score suffered from her erratic credit-card payments. She didn't know how badly until she applied for a mortgage and was told politely that her credit "wasn't great." In order to qualify for a loan with a reasonable interest rate, her mortgage broker had to send a letter to her lender, explaining how Robyn was now vigilantly trying to pay down her debts and improve her credit (which she was). Fortunately, the bank relented and she was able to qualify for a mortgage with a payment she could afford. But she was determined not to let her credit scores slip again.

Always keep a close eye on your credit scores, which have a direct impact on your ability to take out a mortgage, credit card, or other loan and on the interest you'll pay for it. The higher the FICO scores, the better your chances of getting a low-interest loan. And on a mortgage, that can make a big difference: Someone with a score above 760 could literally pay thousands of dollars less per year in interest than someone whose score is below 620. Different credit bureaus can have different, and sometimes incorrect, information. So take advantage of the legislation that now entitles you to one free copy of your credit report annually from each bureau. You can also call your card company to see if it offers free access to track your score. Some credit-card issuers (like Washington Mutual's Providian division) offer free FICO score monitoring services, which provide monthly updates from one of the bureaus, accessible through your account online.

If you do notice changes in your score or report, call the credit bureau that issued the score or report and ask for an explanation. If there are errors on your report, you can submit a request for removal online, citing the reasons for the error, and your report should be corrected (and your score could improve as a result). You can also send a letter using the sample dispute form below as your guide (it's published by the Federal Trade Commission).

Date
Your Name
Your Address
Your City, State, Zip Code

Complaint Department
Name of Company
Address
City, State, Zip Code

Dear Sir or Madam:

I am writing to dispute the following information in my file. The items I dispute also are encircled on the attached copy of the report I received.

This item [identify item(s) disputed by name of source, such as creditors or tax court, and identify type of item, such as credit account, judgment, etc.] is (inaccurate or incomplete) because [describe what is inaccurate or incomplete and why]. I am requesting that the item be deleted or changed [to X] to correct the information.

Enclosed are copies of [describe any enclosed documentation, such as payment records, court documents] supporting my position. Please investigate this (these) matter(s) and [delete or correct] the disputed item(s) as soon as possible.

Sincerely,
Your name

Step Six:

DON'T WAIT TO INVEST

It often doesn't make sense to put every available dollar toward your debt. Sometimes investing some of that extra money can make better financial sense. Maybe you've been able to transfer your credit-card balance or negotiate your rate down so that you're paying just 1.99 percent APR (annual percentage rate), but you can make more than that in interest with a money market account or a CD (or certificate of deposit, which requires a set period of deposit for a fixed rate of return). In the spring of 2008, there were a few one-year CDs available with an interest rate of 3.5 or 4 percent and some high-yield money market accounts were paying up to 3.25 or 3.5 percent (when the Federal Reserve raises interest rates, yields on such accounts can be even higher). Though you want to continue to pay off your debt, you could also put some of your money into an interest-bearing account or CD. This way you'll actually be earning more than you're paying in interest on your debt. (We'll get into more detail on CDs and money market accounts in Chapter Seven.)

You may also want to use some of the money you've saved toward a down payment on a home, instead of paying off a debt. (We'll go into more detail on how much to put into a down payment, versus a debt, in Chapter Eight.) Now that you're on your way to paying down any outstanding debts, it's time to focus on making more money! In the next chapter, we'll explore several ways you can start earning extra income now.

Smart Cookie Summary

Discussion Questions:

1. How do you think you'd feel if your debt was gone? How would that change your life?
2. What kind of "good" debt do you have? "Bad" debt?
3. What's the most you remember ever charging on a credit card? Why did you charge so much?
4. What did you learn from reading your credit reports and checking your score(s)?
5. What are three steps you can take now to improve your credit score(s)?

Smart Steps:

1. List all your balances owed and the interest you're paying on each obligation.
2. Decide on and prioritize your payments based on the amount owed and interest you're paying.
3. Call your creditors and try to negotiate a lower interest rate.
4. Set a date by which you'd like to have each debt paid off completely.
5. Review your credit reports thoroughly and contact the bureaus to correct any inaccuracies.

chapter 6

Make More Dough

Easy Ways to Earn Extra Income

Now comes the fun part. Being financially successful isn't just about finding ways to spend less and save more. We want you to earn more money too! Being a Smart Cookie is all about finding ways to attract more money into your life. We don't mean taking a job you hate because the paycheck's better. We're talking about turning hobbies and passions into money-making opportunities, earning extra cash just by cleaning out your closet or bookshelves, and getting the raise you deserve at work.

Find Out What You're Worth

Before we talk about how to make more money outside your job, let's figure out whether you're earning enough money now *at* your job. Do you know what the average salary is for someone in your position? Or how much coworkers in similar positions are making? Unless you're in HR or you've been job searching lately, you probably don't. It's easy when you've been at one company for a while not to think about how much you're earning—as long as you like your job and make enough money to cover your expenses. It's often not until you learn that a colleague just got a major raise or you look for another job—either because you're unhappy in yours, you're laid off, or you just can't make ends meet anymore—that you focus again on your own income.

The fact is, right now you may be earning a lot less than you could be if you performed the same function at a different company, or even in a different department at the same company. You may actually be entitled to a higher salary in the position you're in right now; you just need to ask for it. Even if you have no plans to look for a new job, it's important to know how your salary ranks compared to industry averages—and to your colleagues, if they're willing to disclose their earnings (some of ours were)—so that you've got more information if you ask for a raise or a transfer.

You can find out what the average salary is for someone in your position by checking with the local chapter of a guild, professional association, or union in your industry. If you belong to a guild or union at your job, check the pay scales and see what the criteria is for moving up to the next level to ensure that you're making the maximum available for your position and are working efficiently toward the next pay grade. Payscale.com offers a free salary-comparison report for your job in your city, based on your experience and education, using information from other anonymous users. You can also get salary information for jobs by logging on to sites like salary.com, workopolis.com, or monster.com. Or go to bls.gov and search by area and occupation to see the average hourly and annual salary of specific job occupations. Keep in mind that salaries vary by city, as does the cost of living.

Get the Raise You Deserve

Many of us were brought up believing that we're supposed to focus on the nonmonetary benefits of our jobs: the fulfillment that comes with improving children's lives as a teacher, the satisfaction of being recognized and praised for a job well done as a manager, the pleasure of throwing the perfect party as an event planner. Sure, such rewards have their place. But there's no reason why you shouldn't be compensated monetarily as well for the valuable services you're providing.

A lot of women have difficulty asking for raises. Maybe we're worried about "rocking the boat" and causing resentment among colleagues or tension with our boss. Or we're afraid we'll be turned down, and then we'll be forced to make a difficult decision about whether to remain in our job. Or we don't place enough importance on the work that we do. We also tend to bring our emotions with us when we enter these discussions and may be apt to take a rejection personally, instead of just focusing on the facts. Whatever the reason—our reluctance to ask for more money is likely one major reason why so many of us are still earning less than our male counterparts.

Women working full-time still earn, on average, about 80 cents for every dollar earned by men in the United States, according to the Bureau of Labor Statistics. The good news is that's up from 63 cents in 1979. The bad news is that the pay gap narrowed less because women made progress than because men's wages fell dramatically, particularly in industries like manufacturing. And though the trend is heading in the right direction, 20 percent is still a significant difference.

One way to close that gap is to make sure you're earning what you deserve. There's no reason why you shouldn't earn as much as your female or male coworkers if you're contributing the same amount to the company. But if you don't *ask* for a raise or promotion, your employer has every reason not to give it to you. Your boss wants to pay you the least amount possible to keep you happy and productive, in order to maintain the bottom line. If you don't speak up, he or she may falsely assume that you're perfectly happy with your small cost-of-living increases or that you lack ambition.

When Katie was just out of school and working at her first public-relations job, she earned about $13 an hour. Though she was working long hours (about ten a day) and earning accolades from her colleagues for her efforts, she was scared to ask for a raise since she had so little experience. Even after her boss hired a new colleague and she learned the new hire was making twice as much as she was, Katie kept putting off her request, hoping that her boss would just give her a raise. When he didn't, she started looking around. It was only after she found a new job that would pay her a base salary of $50,000, or about $16,000 more than she was then making, and told her boss about her new offer that she learned he would have matched that salary to keep her. She didn't make the mistake of waiting again. (We'll have more details on how she successfully negotiated a raise in her next position later in this chapter.)

In fact, three of us have received significant pay increases and/or promotions in the past two years by having the courage to ask for one, being well prepared, and citing our accomplishments. Here's how you can do it in six simple steps:

1. **Determine why you deserve a raise.**
    - Have you exceeded the expectations of your job? Can you cite specific examples of ways in which you went beyond the requirements for your position? You should be able to, if you plan to ask for a raise.
    - Have you had feedback from your manager that you are doing well? Take note of all the positive comments that you get. If you have had rave reviews from your senior managers, then be sure to mention this when you discuss getting a raise. This will boost your evaluation.
    - Do you stay late or come in early? Have you volunteered to cover your colleagues' shifts or come in on a holiday to help out? If you've demonstrated your commitment to the company, make sure to note that during your conversation as well.
2. **Decide what you want and would be willing to accept.**
    - Are you looking for a certain percentage wage increase or a specific amount? Be prepared with both a specific amount and a percentage number. Remember to ask for a little more than you'd accept, as this will be a negotiation.

- Though it will be tempting to ask for a lot initially, be careful. If you ask for too much, you risk being turned down altogether. Be realistic and stay within a range that makes sense for both you and your boss.
- Be clear about what you want and are willing to accept. Would you be happy with an extra week or two of vacation (or other benefits) in lieu of a raise? If your boss offered a onetime bonus instead of a raise, how much would be acceptable? Would you prefer an outright raise or better rates of commission that could bring you more money if you performed well? Make sure you have the answers to all these questions before you sit down with your boss.

3. **Pick the right time.**
   - Be careful not to schedule a meeting with your boss during a particularly busy period or after some bad financial news. Pick a time when you know he or she will be relaxed and in a good mood. Don't schedule it at the last minute, because it will give your boss little time to prepare beforehand and may give the impression you're trying to catch him or her off guard. Give enough advance notice for both of you to feel prepared when you have the meeting.
   - Be aware and considerate of what your boss is going through in terms of pressure at work. If you know he or she is dealing with difficult cutbacks or other stressful situations at work, postpone your meeting until the dust has settled.
   - Pick a time that's opportune for you too, like after you've just successfully completed a big project or had a favorable employee review. It's good to take advantage of the momentum generated by a positive evaluation or the successful completion of a project while it's still fresh in your and your boss's minds.
   - Remember that most companies award raises at the beginning of the fiscal year, after the new budget is approved, but that budget

discussions often begin months earlier. If you want a raise in the new year, you might approach your boss a few months earlier and acknowledge that you are asking for the raise now but don't expect to get it until the next fiscal year. This gives him or her enough time to account for the additional money for salary and wages in the budget to accommodate your request.

4. **Come prepared.**

- Put yourself in your boss's shoes. He or she needs to know what you've contributed to the company to deserve the extra pay. Be ready with a list of your achievements, using the most specific details you can (e.g., how many people you've managed, how much you sold in ads), and be able to explain how each accomplishment benefited the company.

- Have all the documentation you need to back up your request. You have to be prepared to answer questions about the work you've done if your boss brings it up. Have you developed a successful program, won awards for your work, or found a way to increase company revenue? Be prepared with data showing how much you increased revenue or web traffic, for example, or bring printouts of e-mails documenting praise from clients or colleagues about your work.

- Present your case professionally and with confidence. Don't tell your employer that you're struggling to make ends meet on your current salary. This is your chance to explain why you are a significant resource for this company. You need to convince your employer that your contributions are valuable and deserve to be better compensated, not that you simply want more money.

- Keep your cool! Never get angry or present ultimatums, both of which may backfire. You don't want to put your boss in an uncomfortable position or damage your working relationship. If your boss seems reluctant, just gently remind him or her of the many ways in which you have helped the department and the company achieve its goals.

5. **Be realistic.**

- If you are in a job that has fixed pay scales, be familiar with how you can move to the next level. Remember that some positions are locked into a salary or, at least, a salary range—if you are part of a union, for example—so find out what you can do to advance to the next level as quickly as possible. For example, ask your boss what experience is required to be promoted and how best to achieve it. And write down his or her suggestions. That will help you focus your efforts and be better prepared to ask for a promotion later, when you can specifically cite the experience you've gained and the contributions you've made in each area you discussed.

- Also, keep in mind that a $60,000 salary in Phoenix goes much further than the same salary in New York City. Salary scales and rates vary from area to area. Adjust your expectations accordingly. You should be paid not only based on your experience and education but on the cost of living for the city in which you work. This can work to your advantage if you're willing to be transferred to a different office or spend part of your time at a different company location. For example, if you are based at an office in a suburb but are often required to work at a main office in a major city, you can cite the additional costs of commuting and parking when asking for a salary increase. Or if you live in Kansas City, for example, but are willing to relocate to Chicago for a higher-level opening, make sure the accompanying salary increase you negotiate takes into consideration the higher cost of living as well as moving expenses.

- Check to be sure that your company is doing well financially. If it just announced major quarterly losses last week, there's probably not a lot of money available for raises. In this case, you might want to acknowledge the fact that the company may not be in a position to award merit raises at this time but see if you can get additional vacation time or other nonmonetary perks instead and then ask for the raise at a later date.

6. Follow up.
   - If you don't get what you want initially, ask your employer what you could do to boost your chances of getting a raise in the future. Then make sure to cite the improvements you've made in those areas the next time you approach your boss.
   - If your boss decides to review your case and delays a decision, suggest a time frame for meeting again. When you are wrapping up your meeting, be sure to book another one before you leave, allowing for enough time so your boss can make a well-thought-out decision and one that is fair.
   - If the follow-up meeting is scheduled several weeks after the first, check back in with your boss as the date approaches. This will help keep your request in the forefront of your boss's mind and remind him or her that you expect your request to be addressed and resolved.

HOW WE DID IT

Comparing Notes (and Checks) with Colleagues
(Sandra)

When I was offered a promotion at my job, I could not have been more thrilled. It had been only a year since I was originally hired. Since that first day, I dreamed of moving up from the associate to the public-relations manager position. Of course, having the change in title and responsibility was very exciting, but so was the idea of making more money!

I knew I would be sitting down with my boss to discuss salary, and I wanted to go in prepared. I needed to get an idea of what my colleagues in the same position were making—so I asked them. Of course, I had to be careful with this question, and I gave everyone I asked the option of not telling me their salary if they weren't comfortable discussing it. But to my surprise, each colleague I asked was willing to tell me what he or she was making.

I was looking forward to being presented with the salary that I knew my colleagues were making. But when my boss laid the offer in front of me, the $45,000 total—base salary plus potential bonus—was $5,000 below the standard amount my colleagues were making ($50,000). I was taken aback. Since I knew about the discrepancy, I was able to ask my boss why I was earning less than my peers. He explained that, although I had been with the company for over a year working within the public-relations department, I didn't have experience in the manager position, so I could not be paid the full salary right away.

I was not willing to back down without a fight. I told my boss flat out that I knew what everyone else on the team was making and assured him that my contributions were equally valuable. It seemed that my manager was not going to offer me more money right away, but I knew there had to be some wiggle room. I looked at the offer on the table: a base salary of $35,000 with a potential bonus of $10,000 if my team and I met certain targets. By the end of the meeting, I had increased my base salary from $35,000 to $40,000. Clearly my track record in my previous position was an indication of my potential to perform, especially since he was offering me a promotion. So I also negotiated a clause in my new contract that stated that after three months, if I could show that my performance was equal to that of the rest of the team, my base salary would be increased another $5,000 and I could earn a $5,000 bonus too. Three months later, after I had clearly proven that my work equaled that of my colleagues, I went back to my manager and my base salary was increased to $45,000 plus a $5,000 bonus!

Using Outside Offers as Leverage
(Andrea)

The company where I worked had hired me as a marketing strategist on a contractual basis. Since I wasn't sure if my contract would be extended or if I'd be hired full-time after the contract ended, I kept looking for other jobs while I was there. Another company ended up offering me a full-time position with a great package. Once I received the offer, I told my boss about it. Though he knew that I was shopping around, the realization that I had another offer in hand prompted him to take action quickly. He let me know that he wanted me to stay and, within hours, came back to me with an offer for a full-time position with a better title: director of marketing strategy. Once he asked for the specifics of my offer from the other company, I realized the power was in my hands. I was candid about all the details, which were very good (better even than I'd expected), and asked if he could make a comparable offer. He was able to match most of what the other company had offered me. I had a tough decision to make that weekend. I liked the other company but preferred to stay where I was, since I'd already begun building some expertise and contacts. But I had to know if he really thought I would be a good fit in this position or whether he had just offered it because he knew, if I took the other job, I could be gone tomorrow without being able to finish the project that I'd originally been hired to do. I decided to sit down with him and to candidly discuss what I expected in this position, what he expected from me, and what I wanted to get out of it. I'm glad I did. He was very responsive, encouraging, and open. I accepted his offer and had no regrets. The lesson: It never hurts to look around. I learned that my value in the marketplace was higher than I'd imagined, and by having the other offer, I was able to negotiate a better and more permanent position for myself with the company I'd already started working for.

Consider a Career (or Job) Change

It's also important to check in with yourself periodically and make sure that you're still enjoying your job. You don't want to get stuck in a job just because you're used to it, you're afraid to make the switch, or you've convinced yourself that you've already invested so much in this particular career path that it would be foolish to change directions. These are all legitimate concerns. But they're not reasons to stay in a job that doesn't pay you enough to have the life you want or that doesn't give you fulfillment.

If you weren't in your current occupation, what would you love to do? What would be your perfect job? Are you on track to get there? Maybe you've always harbored a dream of becoming a chef or opening your own bed-and-breakfast. There's no reason why you can't start setting the foundation for those plans now by researching how much it would cost to open a bed-and-breakfast, for example, or by taking a cooking class. In fact, you can go one step further and try out your dream job. Websites like vocationvacations.com let you test-drive a new career—for a price, of course. For $549 (as of the spring of 2008), for example, you could get one-on-one training as an innkeeper at a bed-and-breakfast in Oregon, spend a day learning how to be a beer maker at a brewery in Maine, or be mentored by an educator and animal therapist in Florida.

Of course, before you consider a major career change, think about making small changes. Ask yourself: Does your job truly make you *happy*? Could you be doing the same work somewhere else for more money? Would you prefer to work for yourself but in the same industry?

We all asked ourselves those questions, and four of us ended up leaving our jobs soon after—one even made a major career change. Katie, a public-relations manager, realized she wanted a more flexible schedule and wanted to work on a wider range of projects. She started by taking on extra contracting jobs outside her full-time job, providing public-relations services to clients that wouldn't conflict with her job. Once she'd established her reputation and secured some big contracts, she left her full-time job to start her own PR agency. In her first month of being in business for herself, she made $2,000 more than she'd been getting paid at her former job!

Andrea took a new marketing job at a different agency, as she mentioned above, starting on contract and moving to full-time, so she could work on projects she was more passionate about. And she increased her salary in the process. Angela left a job at a TV production company that she enjoyed, but that came with long hours and low pay, after realizing she could find another job profession she felt equally passionate about but that paid a lot better. She wanted to be able to determine her hours and how much she made, so she took courses and got certified to go into business for herself as a realtor. As we mentioned earlier, Robyn got a master's degree while she was working full-time. With her new credentials, she was able to get a new job and double her salary as a social worker. Sandra stayed with the same company but was promoted to a more senior position than when we had first started meeting.

Below, we've shared a couple of our stories about how we made those transitions.

HOW WE DID IT
Becoming My Own Boss
(Angela)

After talking with the other Smart Cookies on a weekly basis about what we all really wanted in life and what our goals were, I realized that while I enjoyed my TV production job, it was not funding my dreams. I had so many other things I wanted to do, and I knew that if I stayed where I was, I would not be able to fulfill those goals. The other Smart Cookies encouraged me to consider all of my options and think about the interests I had aside from my current job, so I could find a career that would be fulfilling and challenging while providing the funds to reach my bigger goals. After the perfect-day exercise, I also realized that I loved having an accommodating schedule and wanted to be more in control of my earning potential. I needed to find a career that would give me flexible hours, creative challenges, and unlimited income potential. Real estate offered all three. It also allowed me the opportunity to help others build long-term wealth—something that was in line with our goals as Smart Cookies.

I went back to school for my real estate license five months after the first Smart Cookies Money Group meeting. I was taking the coursework to obtain my license while I was still working full-time, so evenings and weekends were devoted to studying. I wasn't so concerned about the tuition for those classes putting a strain on my finances—the classes weren't too expensive—but I knew that starting my own business would be costly. And, though I would be working as hard as I could to get the business off the ground, it would take a while to build, so I might not make a lot of money right away. Of course, I had an idea about what the business would be like, since my mom was a realtor for many years, but I also spoke candidly with some local realtors whom I knew in the city to get a true sense of the day-to-day schedules, the average earnings for a starting realtor, and the potential commissions for homes in our area, as well as the pros and cons of the career. This way I had a better idea of how much I had to increase my savings in preparation for changing careers. I knew how much money I should save to get started and about how much I could expect to make initially. After I got my license, I sought out a mentor and joined a team with some of the best in the business so I could learn from them and gain access to more listings. I might make a little less in commissions, initially, but I know I'll gain a lot in experience and also get the chance to benefit from their established reputations.

How to Make More in a Low-Paying Field
(Robyn)

Completing a master's degree program had always been a dream of mine. After my husband and I separated, I decided that the timing was right, since I really needed a higher income now that I would no longer be splitting bills and expenses. Plus, now that I was alone, I knew I could focus on myself and take the time I needed to complete a master's program. I wasn't interested in returning to school full-time, because I wanted to keep working so that I did not incur any debt to complete my coursework, so I researched programs that offered part-time and dis-tance education options. I found a program that offered both, and I com-pleted it in about three years. Though it cost about $15,000, the tuition was spread out over nine semesters, so it broke down to about $5,000 a year. I also took steps to cut other costs. I shared all of my textbooks with a friend, for example, which saved about $250 a semester on books.

Once I enrolled in the program, I stayed at the same job until I realized that I was qualified to earn a higher salary just by being enrolled in my master's degree program, even though I had not yet completed it. I ended up taking a job that paid approximately $20,000 more a year and then started doing contract work for about $10,000 a year. By the time I'd graduated, I had doubled my salary, which more than covered what I'd paid to go back to school—not to mention, I'd completed one of my life goals, of getting a master's degree.

Earn Extra Cash

Now that you've maximized your job earnings, it's time to think about boosting your earnings outside the office. There are so many ways to make more money without making a lot more effort, just by thinking creatively. Here are a few Smart Cookie tips to get you started:

- Clean out your closets. Rather than throwing your used clothes away, why not find them a new home, where they will continue to be loved? Smart Cookies clear out their closets on a regular basis and often sell the shoes and clothing items at a consignment store, on eBay, or on craigslist.org. One of the Smart Cookies makes about $300 at the end of each season and puts that toward new clothes. Katie sold her wedding dress for $800 on craigslist.org. You can do the same with clothes—or toys—your baby has outgrown. Some grow so fast that they never even get a chance to wear all the outfits that their parents bought or received as gifts, and a toy may hardly be used if the baby isn't interested. Another possibility? Donate the clothes or toys to charity and keep the receipt. You can write off the value of your donation when you do your taxes the next year and feel good about helping out those who are less fortunate.
- Clear out the clutter. Here's an incentive to clean up your home: You can get rid of your junk and make money by having a yard (or a garage) sale. Team up with friends, family members, or neighbors

and combine your stuff. Then you'll have extra help running the sale and extra inventory to attract more buyers. And who knows? You might end up swapping items with your friends or neighbors.

- Sell stock photos. If people regularly "ooh" and "aah" over your Flickr pictures, maybe you're destined for photographic greatness—or at least a few extra dollars. It's easier than ever to get your photos out in front of the public. There's a lot of competition, but there's also a lot of demand. Marketing stock photos can be a convenient way for you to build up a secondary income stream. Try Fotolia.com, Dreamstime.com, Shutterstock.com, and bigstockphoto.com to upload and market your photos.

- Rent your parking space. If you pay monthly for a space in a lot or garage, but you know your car will be gone during work hours, you can rent out your space during the weekdays to someone who works near your parking spot. Advertise the space on craigslist.org or in your local paper. Robyn rented out her space and earned an additional $50 per month.

- Rent your home for use as a location for commercials, TV shows, or movies. You can register your home with film studios, production companies, and advertising firms, which maintain lists of properties available for shooting. Check out eHow.com for tips or flip through *Opening Your Door to Hollywood*, a 2006 book by producer James Perry, which offers a step-by-step guide to renting out residential or business locations. Daily rates can range from a couple hundred to more than a thousand dollars (even more if your home is used in a movie shoot). Andrea's friend and her husband had just built their dream home and needed to furnish it, but they were short on cash after finishing construction. They decided to register their home with a production company for use in TV and films. After just two commercial shoots, they'd already earned $20,000! Note: Be sure to ask for a written policy on what the company does in case of any damage to your home.

- Be an extra. If you've seen the Ricky Gervais show *Extras*, you know that jobs for extras can range from print modeling ads to movie shoots. You don't need a Screen Actors Guild (SAG) membership or even any acting experience to qualify—just the patience to sit on a set for hours and the flexibility to try out a lot of different costumes and lines. Pay can range from $100 to more than $1,000 a day. Check out sites like www.extratalentagency .com for more info.

- Help friends find better jobs. Internet sites like H3.com and jobthread.com connect employers with prospective employees, many of whom are already employed and not actively job-hunting, via networking. The rewards for referring a candidate who gets hired range from a few hundred dollars to as much as $5,000. This is a great way to break into the recruiting business, with no overhead. Andrea connected with a recruiter who specialized in marketing. Since she had a lot of connections in that field, she referred many of them to the recruiter. She earned additional money from the referrals and helped some friends land great new jobs.

- Plan that perfect day. If you love weddings, planned your own, and/or have always wanted to plan a friend's wedding, why not do it *and* get paid for it? Many people would hire a wedding planner in an instant but can't afford the rates that a professional charges. Find out what a beginner planner would charge to get an idea of what is reasonable for someone at your level. Once you've built up some contacts, you might also consider party planning in general—first for friends and then for bigger clients.

- Get paid for your opinion. Companies often need focus groups, and market researchers need consumers, to test new items or to share their ideas about new products, shows, or ad campaigns. You can earn $25 or $200, depending on the project and the amount of time required. (Check out research firms in your area for upcoming panels and focus groups. Greenbook.org has a large database of market-researching firms and focus group facilitators, searchable by area.)

- Reap rewards for research. You may have grown up taking the Internet for granted, but there are plenty of people who aren't familiar with it or are too busy to spend time on it. If you're skilled at extracting information through a web search, you can hire yourself out as an Internet researcher for professionals like lawyers and writers. Why not make extra money at something you are already doing? (Check your local classified ads, craigslist.org, or the job postings on mediabistro.com.)

- Be an undercover consumer. Sign up for a secret-shopper program, where you can eat or drink out for free while rating the restaurant, or shop and rate the retailer. You can often bring a friend as well. Three of the Smart Cookies are secret shoppers and have found it to be a great way to eat and drink at some fabulous restaurants for free! Check out sites like www.national associationofmysteryshoppers.org or www.mysteryshoppers america.com for more information. Just note that they each require membership fees—starting at $24.95 and $34 respectively as of mid-2008—to gain access to training and potential jobs.

- Consider contract work. If it won't conflict with your full-time job, seek out freelance or contract work in the same field. By networking, Katie was able to get additional contract work providing public-relations services for clients outside her full-time job, earning an extra $2,500 a month! (Eventually, as we mentioned earlier, she was getting so many referrals and requests for her services that she left her job to open her own PR agency.) Robyn learned about a project seeking registered social workers through the Board of Social Workers newsletter in her area. She was hired on contract for a project in which she made extra money meeting with and interviewing people who wished to adopt children—on her own time, outside her regular job.

Turn Your Pastime or Your Passion into a Paycheck

Do you spend most mornings exercising? Take a basic trainer's course and start training friends and family at your local gym or at home, where you can charge hourly. Not only are you keeping fit but earning extra money while you're at it. Andrea's friend Erin, a preschool teacher struggling on a low salary, turned her passion for fitness into extra earnings by becoming a personal trainer. In a year, she was able to increase her income by 20 percent and stay healthy and fit.

Of course, you don't need to be a fitness trainer, but chances are you already participate in some pastimes that could make you money. In your notebook, make a list of at least five activities that you really enjoy doing, like shopping, knitting, walking your dog, or even drinking wine. Now spend some time brainstorming about ways you could make money doing any of these activities.

If you like shopping, for example, you could earn extra money working as a secret shopper on the weekends. Or you could take a part-time job at your favorite store—many retail stores hire extra employees to help out during the busy holiday season between Thanksgiving and New Year's. Not only will you earn more money but you'll get employee discounts on items you'd probably buy anyway (and save money on holiday gifts). Like knitting? Why not knit sweaters, scarves, or gloves and sell them to friends or give them as gifts on birthdays to save money. If you enjoy walking your dog, ask around to see if your neighbors need their dogs walked. You can make extra money walking theirs as well. Enjoy wine? Look for part-time work at your local wine store, or sign up for wine-tasting classes and see if the instructor needs an assistant at future classes. Many wine shops offer tastings and classes and might be able to use an extra pair of hands in exchange for free wine or a little money. That's exactly what Andrea did. One of her former colleagues started a business that offered wine tastings at company events. Andrea offered to help out. It was a great opportunity for her to make extra cash, sample some wine, and meet new people.

If you enjoy playing basketball or soccer, consider coaching. If you are already taking classes in yoga or Pilates or dancing, consider training to become an instructor yourself. Or see if there are jobs available at the studio on the weekends or evenings—manning the front desk or helping to set up equipment, for example—in exchange for free classes. With a little effort and ingenuity, it's possible to turn almost any pastime into a paycheck.

Smart Cookie Summary

Discussion Questions:

1. Do you know what people in similar positions to yours are earning?
2. Do you think you're getting paid what you're worth?
3. Have you ever asked for a raise? Why or why not?
4. How much do you want to be earning next year or five years from now?
5. Are you happy in your job? Why or why not?

Smart Steps:

1. Find out what the average salary is for someone in your area and position.
2. Review the tips on asking for a raise or promotion. Practice with a trusted friend first and get feedback before you approach your boss.
3. Write a description of your perfect job. How similar is it to your current job? What would you need to do to get there?
4. List three ways you could earn extra income now.
5. List some of your favorite pastimes and brainstorm ways you could earn money for doing them.

chapter 7

Watch Your Dough Rise

Everything You Need to Know about Investing

You don't always have to work for your money. Your money should also be working for you! No matter what your goal—whether you want to be able to take a vacation at a resort in the Caribbean this winter, make a down payment on a three-bedroom home in a few years, or have enough money to retire at 50—there's a type of investment out there that will help you get there faster.

In this chapter, we'll walk you through some basics that every woman should consider, including: contributing to your company's retirement plan, investing in a Roth IRA, and having a high-yield savings or money-market account. Since forming the Smart Cookies, we've contributed more than $20,000 to our retirement and investment accounts and also saved thousands of dollars for short-term goals. Of course, we also consider purchasing your home one of the best investments you can make. Among us, we have invested in close to $1 million worth of real estate. (We'll share how we did it and what to look for in buying a home in the next chapter.)

The Smart Cookie Strategy for Investing

When it comes to investing, we recommend these simple steps. Start by paying off any debt or, at least, paying it down to manageable levels and ensuring that you are making regular contributions into a 401(k) or other retirement plan. Then make it a priority to put aside some money in a high-interest savings or money-market account that you can tap into if you get hit with a big unexpected expense, like a car repair, or if you lose your job. Even if you have a line of low-interest credit or relatives you can count on to help you out in an emergency, it's a good idea to aim for having the equivalent of about three to six months' salary set aside in an accessible account. (If you suddenly lose your job, for example, you don't want to be forced to rely on credit cards and have to worry about covering debt payments while you're unemployed.) Then you can start working toward buying a home, if you don't own one already. One way to do that—and to reach the other goals from your vision board—is by putting money into smart short- to medium-term investments as well.

Investing is an essential part of the overall Smart Cookie strategy for making more dough. But we recognize that with all its acronyms and abbreviations, it's an area of personal finance that can seem complicated, confusing, and—let's face it—boring at times. So we've tried to stick to plain English and focus mainly on specific investments that have worked for us. This is a meaty chapter, so we've broken it into separate sections to make it easier to digest all the information. In the first section, we'll focus on figuring out how much you should invest and then we'll help you decide which options for short-term, mid-term, and long-term investments are right for you.

You probably know that you should invest in more than a home and a 401(k). But maybe you've put it off because you're unfamiliar with other types of investments or unsure of what would fit best with your financial goals. You may be wondering whether you should invest in the markets yourself or whether you need to use a broker or financial adviser. And how much money do you need to invest?

There are lots of common mistakes that women our age make when it comes to investing—from not participating in our company 401(k) plans (women historically have lower participation rates in company investment plans than their male counterparts) to investing in "safe" funds that may offer lower returns because we fear we won't understand more "sophisticated" investment options that may provide higher returns. Each of us definitely held preconceived notions about investing that were holding us back when we first met.

Andrea, for example, didn't realize that the money she put into her retirement plan came out of her pretax earnings, so she could contribute more and feel less of a pinch in her actual paycheck (since some of that money would have been lost to taxes anyway). Angela had been reluctant to put money into her retirement plan because she figured she needed that money now. But once she saw how quickly even small monthly contributions would add up, thanks to compounding, she started putting away $50 a month. It wasn't a lot of money, but it was a good start and it helped her get into the habit of living on less and putting more away for her future. Even if she continued depositing just $600 a year, her contributions could grow exponentially. Here's why:

Three Cheers for Compounding

Remember back in Chapter Five when we explained how card issuers add interest to your credit-card balance each day, so that you are actually being charged interest on your interest? This is why, if you had an 18 percent annual percentage rate and a $100 starting balance but only paid the interest off each month, you'd still pay more than $18 in interest over the course of the year. This can really add up. If you had a credit-card balance of just $500 and paid the interest *plus* 1 percent of your balance each month, it would still take you more than *seven* years to pay off your balance and you'd end up paying another $370 in interest—almost as much as you'd borrowed! When you owe money, compounding—basically, interest charged on your interest—works against you. But the opposite is true when you're investing. Sandra and Angela researched compounding interest as one of their assignments for the money group. What they discovered amazed us all. We were so excited that we raised a glass at the next meeting to celebrate all the money we'd soon be making now that we knew the secret of compounding. Here's what we learned:

When the gains you make on your investment begin to earn money too, and those returns start to earn money, and so on, your results increase exponentially. Even if you contributed only $100 a month and earned a return of eight percent, your investment would balloon to nearly $35,000 in 15 years!

Sure, it takes time for compounding to really work its magic, and if you invest in stocks there's always the risk that they will decrease in value too, so your annual returns may be lower or even negative some years (that's why diversification is so important, but we'll get to that later on). But it truly is amazing how much your money can grow—even with very little effort and no additional deposits.

If you've put off investing because you think you need to have a lot of money in order to earn a lot, we hope we've proven that you don't. Even if you can spare only $25 a month, your first year's investment ($300) can earn you thousands of dollars over the long run. So where should you put your money? That depends on three factors: your age, your goals, and your tolerance for risk. But first let's figure out how much money you're ready to set aside for investing.

Deciding How Much to Invest

When you put together your spending plan each month, think first about putting aside a set amount that you're going to use toward your future. Yes, you have to pay your bills and fixed expenses, but you want to reserve a minimum amount each month to put into investments and *then* start divvying up the remaining funds for your groceries, haircuts, and day-to-day expenses. A great way to ensure that you keep setting money aside for your future is to arrange with your bank or investment firm to have the money automatically withdrawn at the beginning of each month and deposited into your investment account(s) so that you get used to not having that money and adjust your spending accordingly.

By now you should have tried to negotiate a lower interest rate on any remaining credit-card or loan balances. But if you still owe a lot of debt and the interest rate is high (say, 15 percent or more), you may feel more comfortable putting all your extra money toward paying off that balance before you start investing. Think of it this way: If you're counting on annual returns of six to eight percent on your investments but you're paying more than that on your credit-card balance, you're actually losing money each year by not paying off your balance instead. On the other hand, if your credit card's annual percentage rate is low—say, three percent or less—you could even put some money into a high-yield savings account and come out on top. Rates were pretty low in early 2008, but some online accounts offered more than above three percent. And rates fluctuate, so it's good to check current rates as you're deciding what to do. (In the summer of 2007, some accounts offered 4.5 percent or more.) Bankrate.com is a good source for comparing rates for high-yield money-market and savings accounts.

So, how much money are you comfortable taking out each month for investing? Back in Chapter Four, you plugged a number into your spending plan for saving and investing. Is it enough? Take some time and think about how much you really want to set aside to reach your goals (assuming you don't have high-interest balances to pay off). It can be a different amount each month, particularly as you pay off any obligations. You can start with one low amount that you know you can easily put aside for investing next month and then adjust as you go along. The next question is: How do you want to invest it?

Remember in Chapter Three when we asked you to list the big-ticket items from your perfect day and your financial goals? Let's take a closer look at that list. What's the time frame for each goal? And what other, smaller goals would you like to accomplish in the meantime? Maybe you know that three good friends are getting married in the next year, two of them in a different state, and you don't want to go into debt to attend their weddings. Or you want to buy a computer or a new couch for your apartment. Whatever your short-term goals, write them down in your notebook along with an estimate of how much each will cost and when you need to have that money. This will help determine what kind of investments will be the most effective in helping you reach each of your goals.

Short-Term Investing

You probably have some short-term goals you're saving money for, whether it's an upcoming vacation, a wedding, or maybe a class you know you'd like to enroll in next year. Whatever your goal, you're going to want access to your money in a relatively short period: three months, six months, or a year or two. For these time frames, you probably don't want to invest in stocks. You don't want to risk losing any of the money you saved, and you want to make sure that you can withdraw it when you need it. You've got three main options from which to choose. We'll go through the benefits of each so you can decide what's best for you.

Savings account: This is probably the first place you thought about putting that money, and there's nothing wrong with it. It's safe (assuming you put your money in a bank that is insured by the FDIC, or Federal Deposit Insurance Corporation). It's easy to set up and to withdraw money from, and you can even earn a little interest. Traditionally, savings accounts provide very modest returns: from less than one percent to about three percent for high-yield accounts. You might also consider a money-market account. They often offer higher interest rates than traditional passbook savings accounts, but have restrictions on the number of transactions you can make each month and usually require a higher minimum balance.

Money-market fund: Not to be confused with a money-market deposit account, which is like a savings account and federally insured, money-market funds are actually a particular type of mutual fund that is required by law to invest in low-risk securities, like short-term government bonds. Money-market funds usually pay better interest rates than a conventional savings account, but you're assuming slightly more risk. Investor losses are extremely rare, but they are still possible.

Certificate of deposit (CD): When you purchase a CD from a bank or a financial institution, you invest a fixed sum of money for a fixed period of time—like three months, six months, one year, or more. That means you can't touch the money for that period of time. (If you redeem your CD before it matures, you may have to pay an early-withdrawal penalty and/or forfeit a portion of the interest you earned.) In return for leaving the money alone, the issuing bank or institution pays you interest, typically at regular intervals. When you cash in or redeem your CD after the time period ends, you get the money you originally invested plus the interest you earned. This is a great investment to make when you get a big sum of money (say, a bonus at work) and know that you won't need it for a short but specific time period. CDs typically provide the best returns of the three options here and are usually FDIC-insured (up to $100,000 for a taxable account), so they carry very little risk, assuming you purchase one through a bank or reputable financial institution that is stable and unlikely to go bankrupt. The only downside is that, in most cases, you cannot withdraw your money—at least not without the possibility of giving up some returns—before the end, or maturation, date. Once the CD matures, you have ten days by law to decide whether to renew or withdraw the funds. Be aware that banks may automatically roll your CD into a new one if you don't notify them not to do so. Your best bet is often to redeem the CD and then, if you don't need the money yet, shop around for another high-interest CD to invest it in. Also, if you're investing in a variable-rate CD, make sure you understand when and how the rate can change, so you know how much you can expect to earn.

Mid- to Long-Term Investing

Even while you're setting aside money for your short-term goals, it's smart to put some money into mid- to long-term investments as well, even if it's just $25 a month. You can use these investments for a variety of purposes and time frames—withdrawing money or cashing out in a few years if you want to make a down payment on a home, for example, or in a few decades if it's an account set up to help supplement your retirement fund. We'll go through four main categories: bonds, stocks, mutual funds, and exchange-traded funds.

When some of us did research on these and were describing them to the whole group, we decided to use an analogy we could all relate to: our wardrobes. Think of it this way: If these investments are like clothes, bonds would be the basic, if somewhat boring, essentials that you need to build your wardrobe—a plain white button-down, a pair of straight-leg jeans, and other staples that you can count on wearing for years. Stocks would be the more stylish additions that may seem a bit riskier—maybe they'll be out of fashion next year and seem like a bad investment—but also have a lot of upside potential: the sleeveless beaded top you splurged on last summer that became your favorite shirt, drawing compliments from friends and dates. Mutual funds look a lot like your closet should: a mix of basics you can count on and other pieces you're betting will boost the total value of your wardrobe (though there's a risk they may not). So, if one item falls out of fashion or loses its value, you should have plenty of other pieces to offset the loss. Exchange-traded funds are a bit like mutual funds, but they trade like a stock so you can sell them at any time, if the price is right for you. It's like being able to sell all the clothes in your closet to an eager taker who may be willing to buy them for more than you paid. Nice.

Here are more details on each:

Bonds: This is basically a way for companies and state, local, and federal governments to raise money from investors. When you "loan" them the money (a.k.a. buying a bond), you get a record that stipulates how much you paid, a mutually agreed-upon fixed interest rate, how often interest will be paid, and the term of the bond. They're very similar to CDs, except that they can be issued by governments, corporations, and many other types of institutions and are not insured by the FDIC. They're less risky than stocks. But it's best to avoid "junk" bonds. Sometimes called "high-yield" bonds—or noninvestment-grade bonds—these carry a higher risk of default and, therefore, the loss of your investment. If you plan to buy a bond, it's always a good idea to check its rating first. Ratings are issued and published by five major companies: Moody's, Standard & Poor's, Fitch, A.M. Best, and the Canadian-based DBRS. If you're looking for a particular company or governmental entity, you can search the agencies' websites (moodys.com, standardandpoors.com, fitchibca.com, ambest.com, or dbrs.com). Press releases on rating changes from agencies are also reported on all the major newswires, so it's not hard to find them through your favorite search engine by typing in the name of the company and "bond rating." Look for investment-grade ratings of Aaa through Baa (Moody's) or AAA through BBB (S&P and Fitch). Generally speaking, you want to steer clear of bonds that are rated BB or lower, which are considered speculative or junk bonds. Though they may try to tempt you with higher returns, they also carry the most risk of defaulting—in other words, not paying you back on time or at all.

Stocks: In the simplest terms, stocks are a way for you to own parts of businesses. A share of stock represents a tiny proportional share of ownership in a company. As the real or perceived value of the company changes, the value of the share in that company also rises and falls. Investors make money when the share price increases as well as from dividends. These are payments taken from a company's earnings and given to shareholders at regular intervals. (Companies aren't required to provide dividends to common shareholders, but many older companies do.) Some companies, of course, are riskier than others. If you invest in a "blue chip" company—a term given to large, well-established, and well-respected companies like IBM, General Electric, or Coca-Cola—your returns may be lower than if you invest in a smaller, newly public company, like a dotcom, but your risk may be lower as well. It's not likely that any of those three companies would declare bankruptcy. But we all remember the dotcom crash, when dozens of start-up Internet companies went belly up. If you're under 40, we recommend you invest most of your portfolio in stocks. Although there's more volatility (or ups and downs) with stocks, they've historically had higher returns than bonds have. So, if you're not planning to retire for at least fifteen years, you should have enough time to bounce back from any dips in the stocks' value and benefit from their generally higher rate of return over the long run.

Mutual funds: These are a way for you to pool your funds with other investors to buy large amounts of stocks, bonds, or both. Basically, you are investing in a fund run by a professional that, in turn, buys shares of stock and bonds issued by companies and governments. You can buy a mutual fund directly through a mutual-fund company (some of the largest include: BlackRock Funds, Fidelity Funds, and Vanguard Funds), a bank, a stockbroker, or an investment adviser. When you invest in a mutual fund, you are buying shares (or units) of the mutual fund, and any growth in its investments is passed on to you (minus fees and expenses). Each fund manager has his or her own investment philosophy, so shop around to find one that matches your taste and your threshold for risk. For example, some funds mirror popular indices like the S&P 500 (index mutual funds), while other fund managers seek out and invest in companies they think are undervalued or have high growth potential.

Investing in mutual funds has some distinct advantages. The funds often invest in an array of stocks and bonds, so you lower your risks through diversification (while one pick may drop in value, another may do extraordinarily well). Also, you can typically sell your shares quickly and at a fair price if you need the money. Finally, your investments will be monitored by a professional money manager, who should have more experience and expertise—not to mention time—than you do to oversee the investments.

The downside: Mutual funds are *not* guaranteed or insured by the FDIC, so you can lose money investing in mutual funds. Also, you may have to pay charges (like sales or service), fees (up front or when you cash out), and other expenses, regardless of how the fund performs.

The Financial Industry Regulatory Authority (FINRA), the largest nongovernmental regulator for securities firms doing business in the United States, imposes limits on some fees. If you've got a few funds in mind and want to know how the fees and related expenses could affect your return, the FINRA website offers investors a tool that compares the expenses of up to three of the more than 18,000 mutual funds or exchange-traded funds (see below) in its database at: http://apps.finra.org/investor_Information/ea/1/mfetf.aspx. Need some help deciding on a fund? A good place to start is a website like Morningstar.com, which offers ratings and nonbiased general information on a range of funds. You can also check out Yahoo! Finance or other personal-finance sites to find some of the best performers in particular categories—from funds that invest only in health-related stocks to those that invest in a variety of companies that are considered "large-cap" because their overall value, based on their stock price, is typically $5 billion or more. (For more help picking a fund, check out our Smart Bite on the next page.)

Exchange-traded funds (or ETFs): These are similar to the index mutual funds (see above), except that they trade like a stock. What does that mean? The funds track an index of specific sector stocks (buying only shares in biotech companies, for example, or only in companies that make up the S&P 500), but you can actually buy or sell them like a stock throughout the trading day. If you put in a sell order with a mutual fund, for example, you generally have to wait until the end of the day, when the "net asset value" is determined, to find out the price you receive. But with

smart (SC) bite

SIX QUESTIONS TO ASK BEFORE PICKING
A MUTUAL FUND:

1. What are the fees and expenses associated with this fund? There are an array of potential fees and expenses associated with mutual funds, including: sales charges (what you pay to the broker when you buy shares in the fund), redemption fees (which you can pay if you cash in fund shares before a specified period of time), account fees (for maintenance), management fees (paid to the fund manager), distribution/service fees (to cover the costs of marketing and selling fund shares), and other expenses. You should also find out how easily you can buy and sell shares and whether the fund charges a fee for buying and selling.

2. How long has the fund been operating and how has it performed in the past? New or small funds sometimes have really impressive short-term performance records. But because these funds may have invested in only a small number of stocks, a few successful stocks can have a large impact on their performance. As the funds grow larger and increase the number of stocks or bonds they hold, each one has less of an impact on the fund's performance and the overall returns may decrease. So make sure to look at the fund's performance over the long run.

an ETF, you can sell whenever you want and the order will go through in real time, so you'll get the current market price. ETFs even have ticker symbols—some you've probably heard or read about in ads, like the Spider, or SPDR, which tracks the S&P 500, or the Dow Diamonds, or

3. What is the fund's portfolio turnover? The portfolio turnover rate measures the frequency with which the fund buys and sells securities. Why should you care what the turnover is? A fund that rapidly buys and sells securities may generate higher trading costs and capital-gains taxes for you if it's not in a tax-deferred account such as a 401(k) retirement account or an IRA.

4. What is the fund's investment strategy? Remember that funds with higher rates of return may also take risks that are beyond your comfort level and inconsistent with your specific financial goals. Does the fund invest only in high-tech start-ups or does it prefer to invest in solid, well-established companies? Would you prefer a fund that invested only in "socially responsible" companies or one that mirrored a reliable index like the Dow Jones Industrial Average? Decide on a few criteria that are important to you before you select a fund.

5. What services does the fund provide to shareholders? Read the fund's prospectus to learn if the fund provides special services like toll-free telephone numbers and automatic investment programs.

6. How much experience does the fund manager have? Has (s)he managed other funds before, and, if so, how did they perform? What's his (or her) experience and education?

DIA, which tracks the Dow Jones Industrial Average Index. They are easy to buy; you just need a brokerage account. And there's generally no minimum. They can also be more tax efficient than traditional mutual funds because you don't usually pay taxes on them until you sell your shares, hopefully at a profit, and pay taxes on your gains (whereas mutual funds often distribute their capital gains to the investor annually). The downside? It's a passive investment, meaning there's no manager monitoring and choosing the securities in the fund. If the underlying index drops significantly, so will the fund.

Investing Online

You can go to a brokerage office to set up investments in person, but there are also numerous online brokerages—as well as online services offered by traditional brick-and-mortar institutions—that allow you to put money into an account via computer and then buy or sell stocks or other products online (for a fee, of course). These range from no-frills discount brokers like TradeKing or Scottrade to premium brokers like Fidelity, E*Trade, Charles Schwab, or Vanguard to full-service brokerages like Merrill Lynch or Morgan Stanley. As you're deciding where to open an online account, consider what level of service you require and how much money you have to invest. You might start by buying mutual funds through a discount broker, for example, and then as you accumulate more wealth and have other needs, move to a full-service brokerage, which offers a wider and more sophisticated selection of investment products but for a higher price tag. Here are five factors to consider when you begin your search:

1. **Trade commissions and fees:** What will it cost you to buy stocks or other products? Does the fee change based on the type or size of order? Check to see if your online broker offers flat-fee commissions, so regardless of how many shares you buy or the stock price or type of order, you'll pay exactly the same amount every time you trade. Also, be sure to ask about other fees, like minimum balance or inactivity fees. (You may be charged if your account falls below a certain amount or if you don't trade for a certain period of time.)

2. **Customer service:** There are minimum levels of customer service that all brokers should provide. For example, you should be able to contact someone if you have technical or other problems and get help in a reasonable amount of time. But when deciding how much more service you want, think about how often you may want to speak to someone and how much advice you need. If you're considering a full-service brokerage, look at the range of customer services the various firms provide and how much those will cost you. With a discount brokerage, you're largely on your own, though you often have access to research tools. Angela prefers a full-service brokerage because she values the additional advice, while Katie prefers using a discount brokerage in part because she really enjoys doing her own research, using the brokerage site's tools.

3. **Trading tools:** Trading successfully is a lot easier when you have the tools and resources to research the stocks, bonds, or funds you want to buy and to execute your trades quickly and conveniently—or you have a professional adviser providing you with recommendations on what to buy (as at a full-service brokerage). With discount brokerages, you are largely doing the work on your own, but even a low-cost brokerage should give you access to a wide variety of tools to help you make the most of each trade. These can range from access to real-time stock prices and live finance news feeds to sophisticated financial planning tools, fundamental and technical data on stocks and bonds, and market research reports. Ask your broker what tools you'll be able to use for free, based on the account you choose to open.

4. **Account minimums:** Do you have to deposit several thousand dollars before gaining access to cheap trade commissions and trade tools? You may think you signed up for $4.95 trades with a discount broker, for example, until you place that first order and get charged $15.95 because you didn't deposit enough money into your account. Check to see if the price you pay per transaction is the same regardless of how much you have in your account. Some brokers have different tiered

accounts, so that you may pay more per transaction if you have less in your account (or don't agree to make a certain number of trades per year). Keep in mind that the minimum account requirements for full-service brokers, who often specialize in high-net-worth clients, are generally higher than for discount brokers. Also, if you don't have much to invest, your account may not get as much attention from a top-tier, full-service broker as his (or her) larger accounts do.

5. **Investment options:** Both discount and full-service brokerages provide a range of investment products from which to choose, including stocks, bonds, CDs, or mutual funds. Many also offer other options, such as checking accounts and credit or debit cards. Be aware that some brokers may charge more to invest in particular products, so be sure to check what the fee is for each type of purchase.

Really Long-Term Investing (a.k.a. Retirement)

Even while you're investing your money for short- and mid-term goals, you should be tucking away a little bit for retirement—especially if your employer offers matching programs. Here are four different options to help you save for retirement, whether you're working full-time or on contract, or you're self-employed:

- **Individual Retirement Account (IRA):** This is a specialized account that allows you to put some of your income into a tax-deferred fund, meaning you won't pay taxes until you withdraw your money in retirement. These are great if you don't have a retirement fund through your job. Setting up an IRA account can be as easy as downloading the application forms, signing them, and putting them into an envelope with a check to start your account. You can use online brokers like those we named above or open an account at your bank.

A few things to keep in mind: There's a limit to the amount you can contribute to the account each year (in 2008, it was $5,000 for those under 50 and $6,000 for those 50 or older), and when you make a withdrawal, you will be taxed at regular income tax rates, not at the lower capital-gains rates. Also, the IRS won't let you withdraw your money until you're 59^{1}/$_2$ years old, without paying a ten percent penalty in addition to taxes.

- **Roth IRA:** This is a relatively new type of retirement account that differs from the conventional IRA in that you can't deduct the contributions you make from your taxable income. Instead, it offers *total* exemption from federal taxes when you cash out to pay for retirement or even for a first home (IRS rules allow IRA holders to withdraw up to $10,000 penalty-free when the money is used for qualified first-home expenses—just remember you can borrow money to buy a home, but not for retirement and you still pay taxes on that $10,000). A Roth can also be used for certain other expenses, such as qualified education or unreimbursed medical expenses, without paying a penalty if you only withdraw what you contributed. If you withdraw any of your earnings (anything more than what you contributed) before you're 59^{1}/$_2$ years old, though, that amount is fully taxable and may also be subject to a ten percent penalty. Roth IRAs have the same contribution limits but tighter income restrictions than traditional IRAs. (In 2008, you cannot contribute to a Roth if you make $116,000 or more as an individual or $169,000 or more as a married couple.)

- **401(k), 403(b) (the nonprofit version), or 457 (the government or tax-exempt-organization version):** This is a no-brainer, if your employer offers the plan. Contributions are automatically deducted from your paycheck each pay period so you hardly have time to miss that money, plus it's taken out *before* the paycheck is taxed so the government essentially supplements your contributions. Even better, your employer will often match part of your contribution (free money!). You should also have a say in how the money is invested. Most companies will offer a few options and provide you with online access to your account and quarterly statements that are sent to your home so you can monitor it regularly and make changes in allocations as you see fit. Also keep in mind that you can be taxed and penalized if you withdraw this money before you're $59^{1}/_{2}$ years old. (If you're really in a bind, check to see if you can take out a loan against your retirement plan before you withdraw any money. Loans are not subject to penalties, and you can continue to contribute to the plan while you repay the loan.)

- **Keoghs, SEP- or SIMPLE-IRAs, and Solo 401(k)s:** These are known as defined contribution plans, and are the most well-known retirement plans for those who are self-employed or own a small business. They tend to be very flexible in the amount that you can contribute each year. In general, the plans listed above in bold allow you to make contributions of as much as $46,000 in 2008—or, in some cases, a bit more if you're 50 years or older. Contributions are made pretax, reducing your taxable income (in other words, when you pay your taxes next year, you can deduct your plan contributions from your total income so the amount on which you are taxed is lower). Also, your contributions and earnings grow tax-deferred until they are withdrawn, meaning you pay no taxes on them in the meantime.

   A second type of retirement plan for those who are self-employed or own a small business is a defined benefit plan, like a pension, which has an inflexible contribution amount for the life of the plan but can offer large tax deductions. For more information on all these plans and specifics on contribution limits and on the tax implications for you, your family, and your business, consult with a retirement specialist or log on to the retirement section of the IRS website (www.irs.gov).

Depending on your goals, you'll probably invest in a combination of the categories above. Sandra has some of her money in a high-yield savings account, for example, and the rest in a retirement plan that is spread out among different types of investments so that even if she has losses in one area, gains in others should compensate. Her retirement portfolio includes mutual funds that buy bonds, mutual funds that buy North American stocks, and mutual funds that invest in international stocks. Diversification is always a good idea, whether it's in your overall investment strategy or within a particular fund.

Katie and her husband have divided their investments three ways. They put some into specific stocks (the riskiest form of investment), some into a high-interest savings account, and some into their individual retirement accounts. They use the money in the savings account for short-term goals like paying off the lease on their car or for emergency expenses. They knew, for example, that the car lease was going to cost them about $15,000, but the money wasn't due for several months (when the lease ended). As they save for short-term goals, they keep money in a high-interest account so they're earning interest but can still get instant access to it should they need it.

Katie and her husband hold on to their stock-market investments a little longer. The couple uses an online brokerage service tied to one of their bank accounts that charges less than $20 a trade (you can now find some for even less, so shop around). They monitor their stocks very closely and typically buy and hold these investments for at least a year, so any profit they make qualifies for capital-gains taxes (which, as of mid-2008, was 15 percent on profit) instead of being taxed as ordinary income at a higher rate (which happens if the investments are held for less than a year). They try not to sell a stock until it has increased in value by 15 to 25 percent. They invest only a few thousand dollars this way, just in case their investments go down instead, but they enjoy doing the research and gaining more experience investing. Also, they like to bet on young companies that might carry more risk but might also provide better returns. Katie has spent a lot of time researching the sector in which they've invested most of their money (natural resources) and evaluating the companies before they invest in them.

The $16,000 she's got in her retirement account is actually invested in aggressive-growth funds too, which are riskier than more conservative funds

smart **SC** bite

MAKE IT AUTOMATIC: The best way to ensure that you don't spend the money you intend to invest is to have it automatically withdrawn from your account. Start with an amount you're comfortable with now, then increase it as you become accustomed to living on less or have additional funds available to invest. Sandra initially set up an automatic plan with her bank to deposit $100 every month into her retirement fund. When she decided to move in with a roommate and knew she'd have more money available each month, she immediately called her bank to increase that amount to $500 a month. She knew that if she didn't automatically transfer that extra money into her investments, it would disappear on dinners out, new clothes, or unnecessary getaways. It's a relief for her to know that her money is being routed to help fund her future goals instead. And she isn't shy about sharing with us how much her automatic deposits have added up!

but can also provide higher returns. Katie figures that, since she and her husband are still in their 20s, they are young enough to take some risks with their investment choices. Of course, this does not mean that you should always put your money into aggressive growth funds if you're in your 20s, particularly if the risk of its dropping in value will keep you up at night. You need to tailor your investment choices to match your personal tolerance for risk, as well as your age. Katie has a high tolerance for risk, but she does plan to make adjustments to her retirement account each year as she gets older.

In this chapter, we've tried to provide enough basic information so that you can feel confident investing your money. For the most part, you can make and monitor your basic investments yourself. But as your investments grow or become more sophisticated, you may want to hire a financial adviser or a stockbroker to help. Make sure to find someone you trust who really understands your investment goals and time horizon, and be sure to ask about fees and commissions, as well as requesting to see any certificates he or she has and what the certification entailed. Look for a chartered financial consultant (CHFC) or a certified financial planner (CFP). The adviser you select should also be registered with the state or the Securities and Exchange Commission (look up his/her name at www.adviserinfo.sec.gov). The Certified Financial Planner Board of Standards, Inc., also provides a detailed checklist of questions to ask a potential adviser (www.cfp.net).

You can check the background of an investment professional you're considering through the Financial Industry Regulatory Authority's BrokerCheck program on the FINRA website (finra.org). The Securities and Exchange Commission also offers other options for checking out your broker or financial adviser at www.sec.gov/investor/brokers.htm. Generally speaking, you want to hire someone who will not only save you the time and energy it takes to stay on top of your investments but will help you enjoy returns that are better than you would have gotten on your own. If you don't see good returns on your investments, consider finding someone else or managing the money yourself. It also helps to seek out mentors you admire and whom you can trust as you decide on your investment strategy. They can share advice from their experience and expertise, and you won't have to pay for it.

Though you may prefer to spend more time on it, you should need only a few minutes every month to check the progress on your investments and to decide whether to change your allocation (if one investment is doing particularly badly) or increase your contributions. (That's unless you've got an online account that requires a certain number of trades per month.) Then you can just sit back and relax, knowing that even when you're sleeping—and, by now, you should be sleeping much more soundly—your money is working for you!

Smart Cookie Summary

Discussion Questions:

1. What are your short-term financial goals?
2. What are your mid-term financial goals?
3. What are your long-term financial goals?
4. How well do your current investments match your goals?
5. What investment options are most appealing to you now? Why?

Smart Steps:

1. List your short-, mid-, and long-term goals in your notebook.
2. Beside each list of goals, write down about how much money you'll need to achieve those goals and when you'd like to have it.
3. For each list of goals, write down one or two investment options that match your time frame, your tolerance for risk, and the amount of money you need.
4. If you're planning to invest in mutual funds or exchange-traded funds, do some research to determine which funds might provide the best return for your time frame. (Good resources include: Morningstar.com, TheStreet.com, and Yahoo! Finance, among others.)
5. For each of the investment options that interests you, research the banks, fund companies, or investment or brokerage firms that offer those options, comparing their rates, returns, and other features. If you're in a money group, you can each focus on one category of investments and then share what you've learned at the next meeting.

chapter 8

Home $weet Home

How to Get Real Value in Real Estate

We know that buying a home can be intimidating. It will probably be the largest purchase you ever make. But it can also be one of the best investments. Among us, we have invested in close to $1 million worth of real estate, and we've all seen our homes appreciate in value. Sure, the market is not the same today as it was when we bought our homes a few years ago, but over the long term, housing values have historically increased. And that's not the only advantage to owning your home. Here are some others:

- Buying real estate forces you to save money. Preparing now to buy a home is a great way to get into the habit of setting money aside for long-term goals.
- It's the biggest investment you may ever make, but it can also yield the highest returns. Andrea earned more than $120,000 in two years! Of course, a phenomenal return like that is unusual in today's market— at least in that time frame—since the real estate market has softened considerably. Sales of existing homes in the U.S. were down 22 percent and prices of existing homes were down 6 percent between the end of 2006 and the end of 2007, according to data from the National Association of Realtors. But that also means that, depending

on where you're looking, this might actually be an excellent time to buy: foreclosures are up, builders are making deals, and homeowners who are anxious to sell are reducing their prices. (Also, mortgage rates have been coming down again, since the Federal Reserve's series of interest-rate cuts began in the summer of 2007.) Real estate is cyclical. Over the long run, you can generally expect the value of your home to go up.

- Even better, you can enjoy some serious tax advantages when you sell your home. It's one of the few instances in which the government won't tax your profits—up to a point, anyway. As long as you've owned the home and lived in it for a minimum of two years, you can exclude $250,000 of profit (the difference between what you paid for the home and what you're selling it for) from your taxes if you're single, and $500,000 if you're a married couple. In other words, if you're single and buy a home for $250,000 and then sell it after five years for $400,000, you would pay *no* taxes on that $150,000 profit as long as the home has been your principal residence. And this isn't a one-shot deal. You can do this each time you sell a home, as long as you meet the guidelines. (There are some exceptions to the rule, so check with an accountant to be sure you qualify.)

- You have to live somewhere. Why pay for someone else's mortgage instead of your own? When you rent, you're basically paying for the privilege of staying in that space for the next month. Yes, you're generally not responsible for covering the cost of repairs or maintenance, but when your lease is up, you've got nothing to show for it. When you own, part of each monthly payment should go toward your principal (the amount you owe to cover the price of the home when you bought it, minus the mortgage payments you've made) and the other part to cover the interest on your loan, so you're building equity (the current market value of your home minus what you still owe on your mortgage). When the mortgage is paid off, you've actually got something to show for it: a home! And though you are responsible for repairs and upkeep, improvements you make to your home can help boost its resale value.

- Almost anything else that you buy depreciates in value as soon as you purchase it. Your new car is worth less the minute you drive it off the lot. The computer you bought four years ago is nearly obsolete. You'd be lucky to get one-tenth of the price you paid for it. But buying real estate is one of the few purchases you can make in which you're nearly assured that the product you bought will be worth more, not less, in the future—at least, over the long run.

- You can't deduct your rent from your taxes (unless you're self-employed and using it for work space), but you can deduct the cost of your mortgage interest and your real estate taxes from your taxable income, so you pay less in federal income and state taxes. This could actually save you a lot of money each year, since the interest you pay will likely make up most of your monthly mortgage bill, especially in the first few years of your loan. You'll get that benefit only if you pay enough in one year to exceed the standard deduction, but that's not hard to do. Check the irs.gov website for more information.

- It is easier to buy your first place than you might think. And owning your own place will do wonders for your confidence, not just your bank account.

We know firsthand how valuable real estate can be. Four of us have purchased homes, and we have seen our investments appreciate. Yes, the real estate market has declined recently, but that doesn't mean you should put off purchasing a home (in fact, this might be a great time to buy, since prices are low). You just need to plan on staying in it for a while before selling, if you want to make a profit. And make sure to do your research before buying so you know you are able to afford the down payment *plus* the mortgage and any taxes or maintenance fees and that the property you buy is not overvalued and is likely to increase in value (at least, over the long run). In this chapter, we'll give you a checklist to follow before you purchase real estate, and we'll share stories of how we found and bought our homes. Drawing from our own experience and from Angela's expertise as a realtor, we'll also reveal some secrets on how to save money when purchasing a new home, what criteria to look for in buying a home, and what renovations and upgrades are worth making and will bring the most value when you resell.

Before You Buy . . .

- **Know what you can afford.**

Having a realistic idea of how much you can afford to spend—both on a down payment and all related closing costs, plus the monthly mortgage payments—will save you a lot of time and heartache in your search for the right place. Get your finances in order before you start your search, and make sure you speak to a lender to find out exactly what you can afford. If you're trying to come up with an estimate, consider this: Generally speaking, lenders recommend that your monthly housing costs—which include your monthly mortgage principal, interest payments, property taxes, common charges or maintenance fees, and homeowner's insurance—should not exceed 25 percent of your gross, or pretax, monthly income. To figure out 25 percent of your gross monthly income, multiply your annual gross salary by 0.25, then divide by 12. This figure may be even lower, though, if you are carrying a lot of debt. That's because most lenders don't want your total monthly obligations, or the combination or your debt payments and your housing costs, to exceed 36 percent (the Federal Housing Administration's threshold is a little higher, at 41 percent).

So, for example, if you make $50,000 annually before taxes, or about $4,167 per month, 25 percent would be $1,042 while 36 percent would be $1,500. So you would generally want to pay no more than $1,042 in housing costs, assuming you owe no more than about $458 in minimum monthly payments on your credit cards, school and/or car loan, and other legal obligations like child support. If your monthly debt payments are higher, or represent more than 11 percent of your gross monthly income, you should spend less than 25 percent of your pretax income on your housing costs (and pay down that debt!). Note: In very expensive cities like New York City or San Francisco, where real estate prices are much higher than the national average, residents tend to spend a higher percentage of their income on housing. But that doesn't mean you should. If you're living in a high-cost market, it may make sense to rent a little longer—if your rent is less than you would pay for a monthly mortgage for a comparably sized place—and pay off all your debts and save some additional money before you take on a hefty monthly mortgage payment.

Be aware that a big credit-card balance could also limit the size of the mortgage loan that you'll be able to attain. Before you apply for a mortgage, try to pay off as many outstanding balances as possible. That will help improve your credit score and your debt-to-income ratio (or how much you owe each month versus how much you make). Then you may qualify for a lower interest rate on your mortgage, which can save you tens of thousands of dollars over the course of your loan repayment.

Going through the preapproval process with your bank or a mortgage broker is a good exercise to ensure that you'll be able to afford the mortgage payments and related costs. But don't forget to factor in the closing costs and related expenses—like title insurance and application, lender, and document-preparation fees. Keep in mind that lender fees and other closing costs can vary, depending on where you live. In 2007, the average closing and related costs for someone getting a $200,000 mortgage loan in Indianapolis were about $2,339, but someone in New York City getting a mortgage for the same amount paid $3,830—a difference of nearly $1,500. (Bankrate.com provides a good, state-by-state analysis of average closing costs.) And remember: Just because you've been approved for a specific mortgage does *not* mean you need to purchase a house for that dollar figure. The last thing you want to be is house poor (meaning that so much of your disposable income is going toward your house, you can't afford the other important things you want in your life). Once you've calculated the monthly payments you can afford, pick a price range and stick with it.

• **Decide on a down payment.**

How much money do you need to put down to buy a home? Lenders have generally preferred a down payment of at least 20 percent, but that's changing. If you have really good credit, you may actually be able to get a mortgage that covers the *entire* cost of the home, though we don't recommend that. And, after losing billions in the subprime mortgage crisis in 2007 and 2008, few banks are willing to lend the full cost of the home these days anyway. Don't forget that you'll be paying interest on whatever amount you borrow, so the more money you're able to put into a down payment, the better. The difference can save you thousands of dollars in interest.

If you have debt, you may be wondering: Should I pay off my debt first or save some cash for a down payment and buy a home now? Lenders often use debt-to-income ratio guidelines when they're assessing your ability to cover your housing costs. They look at how much of your gross (pretax) monthly income would be used toward housing costs. Then they examine the minimum you owe each month on your credit cards, car or school loans, and other debt obligations. Though the guidelines can be flexible, depending on your credit score, your lender, and the type of loan you are getting, the general rule of thumb is that housing expenses should be no more than 25 percent of your monthly pretax income, as we explained earlier. And your debt payments, if you have any, should not exceed 11 percent of your pretax monthly income. (In other words, the combined cost of your mortgage payment and related costs, plus the minimum monthly payments owed on other debt, should not exceed 36 percent of your pretax monthly income.) Let's take the same example we used earlier. If you make $50,000 a year in salary before taxes (or about $4,167 a month), you really shouldn't be paying more than $458 in monthly minimum payments toward your debt if you are planning to buy a home now. If you owe much more than that each month on your credit cards, credit line, and car or school loans, you probably need to put your money toward your debt now and postpone buying real estate until you've paid down some balances. Otherwise it will affect the amount of money you'll be qualified to borrow, and could affect the interest rate you are charged on your loan. On the other hand, if you make $50,000 a year before tax, and the minimum payments on your debt add up to about $200 a month or less, it might make sense to buy your home now and put any extra savings you have toward a down payment (though you should still have a plan in place to pay off your debt, of course). You want to try and put down 20 percent on your home.

Why aim for 20 percent? Many banks will allow you to put down less than that on a home, but if you do so, your lender will likely require you to purchase private mortgage insurance (or PMI). This protects the lender just in case you default. By law, your lender should tell you at closing how many years and months it will take you to pay down your loan enough to cancel the mortgage insurance (if you have a fixed-rate mortgage). PMI costs vary from one mortgage insurance firm to another and will depend on the amount of your loan and down payment and your credit score. Your mortgage broker should be able to provide you with specifics.

- **Consider co-owning.**

If you can't do it alone, don't! Buy with a friend or family member or ask your family to help with the down payment. You can arrange it so that you repay them the amount plus a fixed amount of interest over a set time period. Andrea's parents and her uncle offered to help her with the down payment on her first home. They gave her a loan and wrote up a contract agreeing not to charge her any interest on it for the following ten years. Andrea was fortunate that home values were rising remarkably fast in her area at that time. She was able to sell her home after just two years and make enough of a profit to pay her relatives back in full and still have a lot of money left over.

Another option is to agree to pay your friend or relative what you bor- rowed plus a percentage of any increase in the home's value over a set period of time. That way, if prices drop after you buy your home—as they have in most regions of the country in 2008—you'll owe less. If prices increase, you'll owe more; but your home will be worth more too, so you'll still make a profit if you sell it. Of course, a loan from a family member or friend may require no interest payment (or any repayment at all, if they decide to give it as a gift). But whether it is a gift or a loan, always approach your friend or family member(s) with a well-thought-out payment plan. If you are expected to pay them back, it's a good idea to put the terms in writing to avoid potential misunderstandings. If no repayment is required, be aware that under IRS rules you may be taxed on any amount above $10,000 that you get from one person.

- **Research real estate values.**

Can you be sure that real estate values will increase in your area? No—at least not at the rate they'd been growing in some places. After climbing steadily for years, U.S. home prices started slipping in 2007. By February 2008, the average price of a single-family home in the U.S. had fallen to $241,900, down nearly 12.5 percent from the previous summer, according to the National Association of Realtors. The median sale price of an existing single-family home in Las Vegas, once one of the nation's fastest-growing cities, fell nearly 13 percent between the end of 2006 and the end of 2007, thanks in part to overbuilding and speculation (many people had bought homes as investments, not residences, which also helped increase the inventory of unsold homes). Prices fell even further in other areas during the same period: 18.5 percent in the Sacramento area, 19 percent in Lansing, Michigan, and 12 percent in Orlando, Florida. Looking at figures like that can be scary for anyone who's thinking about buying real estate, and we are certainly not recommending that you buy a property now with the intent of making a quick dollar.

But don't be scared by the drop in sales if you're planning to stick it out for the long term. In fact, this can be a great time to buy. In many areas, owners who need to sell may be willing to accept bids that are significantly lower than their initial asking price. If you see a home you love that's been for sale for months, you may be able to negotiate a price that's thousands of dollars lower than the one listed. Just make sure to check the recent sales prices of other homes in the area to ensure you're not paying more than market value.

Remember, real estate markets are cyclical; but over time, on average, housing prices have historically gone up, not down. Hold on to your home for a while and you're still likely to see the value appreciate.

- **Look for a good location.**

As you explore the neighborhood and surrounding city, ask yourself: Is it reasonable to expect that this community will still be an attractive place to live in 5, 10, or even 15 years? Is it an up-and-coming area or an established community? How well is it maintained? Are the streets well-lit and well-paved? Are there public parks? How do graduation and college-acceptance rates and test scores in the local school system compare to those in nearby districts? (Even if you don't have kids, schools play a big part in the resale value of a home.) How do the local crime statistics compare to the national average and to other nearby communities? In addition to residential neighborhoods, does the community have an appealing mix of commercial and business development? Are there local restaurants and shops you'd be proud to show off to houseguests? Are there basic services nearby like a dry cleaner, grocery store, and pharmacy? Check into development plans around your property. Are there many empty lots? Are there plans for more homes or nearby restaurants or other attractions? You can answer these questions by driving around the area, looking up the city's website, and talking with your realtor and with residents who live in the area. You should also talk to a realtor about which of these criteria tend to be most important to buyers in general, so you get an idea of how these could affect the value of the home you buy in the future.

- **Take taxes into account.**

Property taxes may be higher in one community than another nearby. While higher property taxes can often mean newer schools, well-maintained roads, and better community services, prospective buyers may be turned off by them, particularly if neighboring areas have lower taxes. Don't forget to figure taxes into the equation when you're calculating how much you can afford. And talk to your realtor about whether the amenities are worth the higher taxes.

• **Scope out the site.**

If you're buying a house in a typical neighborhood, look for a lot that's square or rectangular, not oddly shaped. It should also be as level as possible. Examine how the home is situated on the lot. Is there enough space between it and neighboring homes? Is the yard large enough for kids or pets to play?

If you're buying a condo or apartment, look at how well the building is maintained and where the unit is situated. Is it facing a busy street or an inside garden? What kind of sun exposure does it get? Is it on the ground floor or upper floors? Ground units that face a street may be less expensive, but they are also more exposed.

You certainly want to make sure that the condo, apartment, or house that you purchase meets your personal needs but also that it will be appealing for potential buyers in the future should you decide to sell it.

• **Remember, size matters.**

But not in the way you think it does. If you're concerned about resale value, you probably do *not* want to buy the largest home in the neighborhood. If most of the nearby houses are smaller than your house, they can actually drag down the value of yours. On the other hand, if you buy a house that's small- or medium-size for the neighborhood, the larger homes around it can help pull up the value of yours. If you want to make sure that your home appreciates, it's smarter to buy a smaller home in a better neighborhood than to buy a bigger one in a less desirable neighborhood. Houses with three or four bedrooms and two or two-and-a-half bathrooms are typically the most smart $\mathcal{SC}$ bite

LOW-MAINTENANCE LANDSCAPING: If the last owner spent a lot on landscaping, they'll likely try to tack that onto the price of the home. And don't forget to factor in the money and time you'll need to maintain it. Unless you enjoy spending hours on yard work, you'll get the best value—and more time to yourself—if the house has low-maintenance landscaping. You can always improve it by adding inexpensive touches, like bushes or flower pots.

popular among home buyers, so if you can stick in that range, you should have more potential buyers when you resell.

- **Focus on features.**

Know which features can improve a home's resale value (and which won't) and which features you can and can't live without.

When Andrea was deciding which condo to purchase, for example, she narrowed it down to one that had a walk-in closet in the master bedroom and a conventional kitchen and another with granite countertops and stainless steel appliances in the kitchen but little closet space. Both the walk-in closet and fancy kitchen would be attractive to future buyers, if or when she chose to resell her condo, but Andrea decided that having the larger closet was more important to her than having stainless steel appliances. An up-to-date kitchen helps boost a home's value, but if you plan on living in your home for a while, you may end up renovating the kitchen anyway.

So it may make more sense to buy a home with an outdated kitchen. You should be able to get a better price, and then you can use some of the savings to make renovations and install new appliances. (That way, you'll have a personalized kitchen *and* a house that's worth more!) Garages also add to the resale value (try to get a two-car garage). And hardwood floors can also make a home more valuable, as long as they're well-maintained. A 2007 report by Hanley Wood LLC, a media company that serves the housing sector, and *REALTOR* magazine found that kitchen remodeling was the best value among indoor renovations last year, returning 83 percent of the costs on average (meaning that if the kitchen upgrade cost $10,000, it boosted the home's value by $8,300).

smart bite

STAGING: Never underestimate the power of a first impression. Buyers usually get a feeling about a home within the first few minutes. If you do resell, "staging" your home can help you boost its value without costing you much but a few hours of your time. Staging is a term realtors use to mean presenting your home in its best, most appealing light. This can mean investing in small touches, like a new tablecloth or shower curtain, giving the bushes in the front yard a good pruning, or maybe adding a fresh coat of paint to the front door, an attractive potted plant on the porch, or a vase of fresh flowers in the entranceway. It's equally important to make sure the house is clean and clutter free. Deciding what to keep and what to let go of is often the hardest task for homeowners. Sandra, who has helped stage friends' homes, offers these tips: *Visualize:* Try to imagine the home as a blank slate. Ask yourself: What would you put in each room if you were to buy the home empty now? Think of how you would want each room to look. Cozy? Chic? Sophisticated? Of course, it's also

If you're buying a condo or apartment, there are other considerations that might be important to you. If you're buying a unit in a large building, consider: Does the building have a doorman, an elevator, extra storage, or access to common areas like a roof deck or garden? It's important to figure out both what matters to you and what may affect the value of your unit. Maybe you're willing to forgo an elevator for a better-priced condo or one with a nicer view. But keep in mind that even if you're fit enough to climb four flights of stairs every day, prospective future buyers may not be.

important to remember that buyers want to imagine themselves living in your space, and they may not share your taste. Just because you want to paint a wall hot pink doesn't mean they will. So try to stick to neutral colors and furnishings, and don't overwhelm potential buyers with photos, trophies, and other personal items. *Assess:* Once your vision for a room is set, you can assess items according to whether or not they fit into the theme. Other questions to ask when it comes to deciding what to throw away are: When did I use it last? Is this a duplicate? Does it hold sentimental value? *Take action:* Once the decision has been made about what stays and what goes, categorize the items into piles: items for storage; items for donation; items for recycling; items for resale; and items for the garbage. Bonus: You can earn extra money through this process by reselling some of your furnishings at a furniture consignment shop, through craigslist.org or local classified ads, or at a yard or garage sale.

- **Find the right realtor.**

It's important to take the time to find a realtor who really understands your financial situation, your timeline, and the qualities you're looking for in a home. You want someone who will work with you through every step of the home-buying process, representing your interests and getting you the best deal possible on the home you want. You want someone who knows the area well and will lend their experience and knowledge to help narrow your search for the right home, who will empower you to make confident and well-informed decisions, and who will support you in your personal and financial goals. It's a good idea to get referrals from friends or family members who have bought or sold a home recently. If you opt to use the Internet instead to find a realtor in your area, seek out well-established real estate companies, then look up profiles of individual agents until you find one who seems like a good fit. You can also ask for references from previous clients. Keep in mind that not all real estate agents are realtors. In addition to being licensed to sell real estate, realtors must belong to the National Association of Realtors and pledge to abide by its code of ethics, a comprehensive list of 17 articles detailing several standards of practice that go above and beyond those required by law—like discussing any financial benefit they might receive from recommending related products or services and sharing all the pertinent facts about a property with all parties (even if it means telling buyers about problems with the seller's home).

- **Look for undervalued properties.**

Before you start looking for a home in a particular area, do some research on median (average) home prices so that you'll be able to recognize an undervalued property. Every quarter the National Association of Realtors publishes on its site, www.realtor.org, median prices for single-family homes in nearly 150 of the nation's biggest metro areas. You can also check the federal government's Office of Federal Housing Enterprise Oversight's House Price Index, which includes separate house-price indexes that reveal overall trends in housing prices for several major metropolitan areas (http://www.ofheo

.gov/hpi.aspx). Foreclosed properties can offer a good value (just be sure to check the criteria we listed above). They can be found in many neighborhoods at below-market prices and are listed in local newspapers. The Department of Housing and Urban Development (www.hud.gov), Fannie Mae (www.fanniemae.com), and Freddie Mac (www.freddiemac.com) all also have links to listings of foreclosed properties. Don't be turned off by problems that are easy and inexpensive to fix, like a room that needs a new coat of paint, a carpet that needs to be shampooed, and dingy curtains or rugs. They can make a home less attractive to buyers and result in a better deal for you.

Katie and her husband picked their condo because it was in one of the most desired neighborhoods in their city, with a low crime rate and short commuting time to downtown offices and within walking distance of parks, restaurants, and other attractions. They also figured the condo was underpriced because it didn't come with a parking spot, and they found that its price was in fact lower than similar listings nearby. But there was inexpensive parking very close by, the building was new, and the condo had two bedrooms and two bathrooms (while much of what they'd seen in their price range had only one bedroom and one bathroom). They realized that not having a parking spot would mean that if they resold the condo, they couldn't charge as much as other units in their building that came with a spot. But the price they paid was low enough that they were confident the value of their condo would increase enough to compensate over time. Indeed, since they bought it in late 2004, their condo has increased by $200,000 in value. That's not a typical rate of appreciation—certainly not in 2008. But it's reasonable to expect that if you buy a home or condo in a desirable neighborhood that costs less than nearby listings, the value of your home is going to go up over time.

Another question to ask yourself before you shop for a home is: Are you planning to buy now and then move in to a larger place in the next few years? Or, are you buying for the long term?

Andrea wanted to live downtown but couldn't afford to buy there initially. So she bought a condo in an attractive suburb, where prices had been steadily increasing. She planned to live there for a few years and then, if the home had increased enough in value to earn her a profit, she would sell it and move into the city. She was fortunate to buy in the midst of the housing boom in her region. In just two years, the value of the first property that Andrea bought increased $120,000. She used some of the earnings from selling the first condo to buy one downtown in a neighborhood she loved, which was also closer to her job. She's now able to walk to work, which has saved her money on gas, parking, and car repairs. Plus, she'd built up so much equity in her condo by 2007—about $150,000—that she was able to increase her mortgage loan and pay off all her credit-card and credit-line debt. Returns as good as Andrea's are unlikely in the 2008 market. But it's smart to keep an eye on home values in your neighborhood to take advantage of rising prices. You can track the market value of the home you buy and others in your area through sites like Zillow.com or Yahoo! real estate (http://realestate.yahoo.com/Homevalues) or by checking listings for prices of nearby homes for sale. If comparable properties are selling for a lot more than you paid, you might consider selling yours and purchasing a home that's either less expensive (so you can keep the profits from your first sale) or upgrading to more desirable accommodations. Just make sure not to overextend yourself, and look for a listing that's a good value for the neighborhood.

- **Pick the right mortgage for you.**

There are two main types of mortgages: fixed rate and adjustable rate. Many people use a fixed-rate mortgage, in which the interest rate stays the same for the term of the mortgage. They typically stretch over 30 years, though many banks offer 15-year mortgages, which is a great way to lower the total amount of interest you'll pay (though it also means higher monthly payments). The advantage of a fixed-rate mortgage is that you always know exactly how much your mortgage payment will be so you can incorporate that into your spending plans.

With an adjustable-rate mortgage (ARM), your interest rate and monthly payments are usually lower initially than they would be with a fixed-rate mortgage, but after a set period they adjust. Depending on the type of adjustable-rate mortgage you get, there will generally be a fixed period of anywhere from one month to five years or more before the rates start adjusting. After that, they either adjust every six months or annually, depending on the loan. A one-year ARM, for example, would begin adjusting a year after you got the mortgage and then adjust again annually for the life of your loan. A commonly advertised hybrid ARM, called the "5/1," would give you a fixed rate for five years (the top number) and then adjust every year (the bottom number). (The Federal Reserve Board provides a good guide at: http://www.federalreserve.gov.) Your interest rate is tied to a financial index, such as the U.S. Treasury Securities index or the London Interbank Offered Rate (LIBOR): If the index is up during the period in which your mortgage adjusts, your rate goes up as well. If it goes down, so does your rate.

The advantage of an adjustable-rate mortgage is that the initial interest rate tends to be lower than that of a fixed-rate mortgage. But, as many homeowners have discovered, if the rates go up a lot as the mortgage adjusts, you can be caught in a dangerous situation. One reason the foreclosure rate in the U.S. has hit record highs recently is that many homeowners got adjustable rate mortgages between 2001 and 2004, when interest rates were extremely low, and convinced themselves that they could afford a more expensive home since the initial monthly payments were so manageable. But by 2006, interest rates had risen considerably, so when their mortgage rates adjusted, their monthly mortgage payments were suddenly much bigger than what they had gotten accustomed to paying. Some people were unable to afford them anymore. You don't want to get caught in this situation, so make sure that you've got enough income or money in the bank to cover any future increase in your monthly payments if you opt for this kind of mortgage.

Make sure to ask your mortgage broker about both the periodic-adjustment cap (the maximum amount your interest rate can adjust up or down from one period to the next) and the lifetime cap (the maximum smart SC bite

WHAT IS A JUMBO MORTGAGE?

If you're buying an average-size home in most parts of the country, you are unlikely to need a jumbo mortgage. But if you're buying an expensive home or if you live in a high-cost area, you may. A jumbo mortgage is one that exceeds a specific amount set by the Office of Federal Housing Enterprise Oversight, which oversees Freddie Mac and Fannie Mae. Initially, for 2008, the limit for a single-family home, apartment, or condo was $417,000 within the continental U.S., or $625,500 in Alaska, Hawaii, Guam, and the U.S. Virgin Islands. However, in early 2008, in an effort to boost sagging real estate sales, Congress authorized the agency to temporarily raise the limit as high as $729,750 in several markets that were designated "high-cost areas"—from Napa Valley, California, to New York City—for loans that originated anytime before the end of 2008. (For a list of cities and counties included and their new limits, check the Office of Federal Housing Enterprise Oversight website: ofheo.gov.)

It's smart to stay under this limit when applying for a mortgage, if you can. Why? Rates on jumbo mortgages tend to be at least one-half percentage point higher than comparable mortgages—and sometimes more than that. In late May 2008, for example, bankrate.com reported that the average national rate for a regular 30-year fixed mortgage was 5.81 percent, while the average rate of a *jumbo* 30-year fixed mortgage was 7.03 percent. Over time, that 1.2 percent difference can add up to thousands of dollars more in interest payments.

percentage that your interest rate can increase over the life of your mortgage). This way you can calculate ahead of time what the maximum monthly payments could be in the future and make sure you can afford them. And remember, it's always best to buy a home that costs *less* than the amount you're qualified to borrow, so you've got a cushion.

When you calculate how much you can afford to borrow to buy your home, keep in mind that most mortgage loans have four parts:

1. The principal: the repayment of the amount you actually borrowed.
2. The interest: an additional payment to the lender for the money you've borrowed.
3. Homeowner's insurance: an amount to insure the property against loss from fire, smoke, theft, and other hazards (required by most lenders).
4. Property taxes: the annual city/county taxes assessed on your property, divided by the number of mortgage payments you make in a year.

There are several benefits to owning your own home, even if the market isn't as hot as it was a few years ago. If home values are increasing in your area, buying real estate can provide a sizable return on your investment—more than you're likely to make by investing in the stock market or socking away your money in a savings account. Even if the market is slow in your area, it's important to remember that, over the long term, you can generally count on your home increasing in value (and if prices have fallen considerably in your city, now may be a great time to get a bargain). Of course, whether you should consider buying now or wait until later depends on various factors—from how much money you have saved to current mortgage rates and market conditions. But even if you're not ready to buy, it's not too early to start setting money aside to purchase a place in the future. As we mentioned earlier, buying a home may be the most expensive purchase you make in your lifetime, but it can also be the most rewarding—as long as you do your research and have realistic expectations. Remember: Ultimately, this isn't just an investment, this is your home.

Smart Cookie Summary

Discussion Questions:

1. When would you like to buy a home?
2. What price range do you think you'll be able to afford when buying a home? (Use the 29 to 41 percent range as a guide.)
3. How much money do you estimate you'll be able to put toward the down payment?
4. What features are most important to you in a home?
5. What are market conditions like in your area now? Are they likely to improve?

Smart Steps:

1. Figure out how much you will be able to afford for a down payment and monthly mortgage, maintenance, and tax payments when you're ready to buy. (This is a good time to consider whether to ask a friend or relative to help out.) Then use that to determine a price range for homes you can afford.
2. Scout out different neighborhoods and homes for sale, and talk to friends to see what they like and don't like about living in their neighborhoods, to help you determine where you want to live and why.
3. Make a wish list of everything you want in your new home, and prioritize it (just in case you can't find a place that has all the features and amenities you want).
4. Research and compare different mortgages. Select one that you feel best suits your financial situation, risk tolerance, and financial goals.
5. Find a good mortgage broker and realtor.

chapter 9

Join the Group

A Step-by-Step Guide to Starting Your Own Money Group

You don't need to be a member of a money group to be financially successful. But money groups are a great way to achieve your goals and strengthen friendships—or create new ones—along the way. We've become best friends since March 2006, when we started meeting, and we're convinced that we've been able to accomplish more together than we would have on our own.

Money groups keep you motivated, accountable, and on track to reach your goals. Plus, sharing such intimate details about your finances and your dreams helps to create a bond with other money-group members that can last a lifetime. It's rewarding to celebrate the progress your fellow money-group members have made and to know that you've played a part in it. It's a relief to have friends you can count on to help you reach your goals. And it's gratifying to be able to share your successes with other women who know, *really know*, how far you've come.

Creating a group isn't hard. Here are some simple steps to get started.

WHO

Be selective in whom you choose to be a part of your money group. These should be people you respect and with whom you want to grow. They should truly want to make improvements in their finances and to learn more about saving, investing, and attracting more money into their lives. They must be committed to their own success and to the success of the other money-group members. And they should be committed to attending all the meetings. These should also be people you trust to maintain confidentiality about the financial information each of you is sharing. Don't just consider how potential members will get along with you but how they will get along with one another as well. Avoid naysayers, gossipers, and anyone who doesn't seem serious about taking control of their finances. Ask yourself:

- Do you share similar values with the members? Make sure the members' motives for joining are similar to yours. Money groups aren't intended to be an excuse to get together and gossip or to grouse about your financial problems. Sure, you can spend some time socializing during the meetings (we always do), but the groups are intended to help you take action to improve your financial situation.

- Do you all have similar lifestyles? If one member is required to travel several times a month for her job, for example, it may make it difficult for her to attend meetings. Or, if some members have kids while others are single, it may make sense to split the group into two—one for parents and one for those without kids—since each group will have unique financial challenges and time commitments.

- Do you have comparable financial goals and challenges? One person might be more interested in sophisticated investing strategies, for example, while another wants to know how to get rid of her credit-card debt. Again, in a case like that, it might make more sense to form two different groups: one dedicated to investing and one that focuses on getting out of debt (though it may also discuss investing).

- Are you in the same or related professional fields? You don't all need to be coworkers or colleagues in the same profession, but it may be helpful to include people who are in the same, or at least similar, industries—particularly when your group starts discussing how to earn additional income, ask for a raise, or consider a career change. You'll be better able to discuss questions about salary ranges, career tracks, and job opportunities. You can also provide one another with contacts and—who knows?—you may even decide to go into business together.

WHAT

Remember that the purpose of a money group is to meet with a group of like-minded people to set and reach financial goals and to provide support and accountability.

- Stick to an agenda of key items. (Check out our Smart Cookie summaries at the end of each chapter for exercises and discussion topics you can use at your meetings. You can also get a sample agenda on our website.)
- Establish ground rules. These should be agreed upon at the first meeting.
- Assign tasks at each meeting. For example, one person might be in charge of keeping minutes, while another is charged with bringing refreshments. Ensure that at the end of each meeting, each group member has a specific assigned task or item to work on for the next meeting.
- Hold members accountable. All members should complete the exercises outlined in each agenda and be prepared for each meeting. And they should be punctual. Your time is valuable.
- Treat the money group like a business, and you'll get more accomplished. Leave some time for eating and socializing, then agree on a time when you'll call the actual meeting to order.
- Pick a leader or a chairperson for each meeting. The Smart Cookies opted to rotate the position for each meeting. But if one member has

particular expertise, and the skills and the time to do so, it may make more sense to allow her to run all the meetings.

WHERE

- Pick a central location that works for every member of the group.
- Look for a space that's comfortable for everyone and that will be available when you need it.
- Try to avoid public places like restaurants, as there isn't much privacy and the noise and other patrons may be distracting.
- You may want to rotate the location—holding meetings at each member's home, for example.
- Always agree on where the next meeting will be held before you adjourn.

WHEN

- At your first meeting, decide how often you want to continue to meet as a group. You can meet as frequently as you want, but we recommend meeting at least once a month. We decided to meet weekly. But even meeting every two weeks can give members enough time to prepare for the next meeting but not allow so much time to pass that it's difficult to pick up the discussion where you left off or to maintain momentum.
- Try to stay with the same time and day for meetings, so they become part of each member's regular schedule.
- Decide on a time frame—from 7:00 p.m. to 9:00 p.m., for example—and stick to it.
- Block out time in your calendar each week or every other week, depending on how often you meet—not just for the meetings but also to work on money-group matters.

WHY

By now you should have a pretty good idea of the reasons why you might want to form a money group. But, just in case, here are a few we've found to be true from our own experience:

- You'll learn to face your fears about money and to overcome them.
- You'll be more motivated and prepared to fix your finances.
- You'll learn more than you ever imagined about managing—and making more—money.
- You'll reach your goals faster.
- You'll have a support system to help you through the rough spots and to celebrate your successes.
- You'll form lasting friendships.
- You'll feel empowered to take control of your finances *and* your destiny!

Preparing for Your First Meeting

As we mentioned before, some of us had not even met face-to-face before we formed the Smart Cookies Money Group. So, of course, we were a little wary about divulging the details of our finances. It's scary to share that kind of information with a total stranger. But each member of the group had been referred by someone else, and each of us made a commitment that first night to be honest and candid about our own finances and to keep others' financial details between us, unless we agreed otherwise. (When we decided to write this book, for example, we all agreed that it would be beneficial to disclose the details about our circumstances.) Before that first meeting, we had never shared information with *anyone* about how much we owed, earned, or spent.

There's a good chance that you haven't either. That's why it's so important that you choose the members of your group carefully and that you make sure that each person is fully committed to improving her finances, attending the meetings, and keeping everything you talk about at those meetings confidential. In order for a money group to work, you need to create an atmosphere of trust and support at every meeting. Each member should feel comfortable sharing the details of her situation, knowing that the other members will listen to what she has to say with respect and understanding.

We also recommend that you make some preparations before you meet for the first time. Decide on the meeting place and on a time and day that works for everyone beforehand, so you can keep the same schedule for future meetings, and figure out about how long you'll meet for the first time so you can plan accordingly. And don't forget the refreshments! It's great to have snacks and drinks on hand. It also helps to give each member a specific task before the first meeting. Decide who will lead the first group, who will provide the food or refreshments this time, and who will take minutes at the meeting. We like to rotate the responsibilities so everyone feels like she is contributing the same amount and we each have opportunities to lead a meeting.

What to Bring to the First Meeting

1. Refreshments. You don't want to have a formal dinner, which could distract from the purpose of your meeting. But consider serving sandwiches, cheese and crackers, fruit, or other foods that are easy to eat with your fingers and not too messy, so that you can enjoy them in a more casual setting and start the meeting while you're eating. If you drink alcohol, having wine or beer on hand can definitely help break the ice (in moderation, of course). Having a glass of wine helped us loosen up in the early stages and feel a little more comfortable with one another. While one person may be in charge of buying the refreshments, everyone should contribute to the tab. Our goal has

always been to try and keep costs to $6 or less per person for food and refreshments. For us, that meant a total of $30, which easily covered the cost of pizza, sandwiches, or other take-out options. We often put any leftover money toward drinks or brought wine that we had at home already.

2. A notebook. You should each have a small notebook that you can use for the various exercises and to take notes during the meetings. It's also a good idea to have one large notebook or binder in which you keep official minutes of the meetings and other resources that you want to share, like printouts of interesting articles or copies of pages from books you've read that relate to the meeting topics.

3. A list of goals and potential meeting topics. Before you meet for the first time, think about what you hope to get from this experience. What are your personal goals for the money group? Why are you joining? What do you need from the other members in order to reach your goals? Write down some topics that interest you. Do you want to learn more about buying real estate, trading stocks, or paying off your debt faster? Are you hoping to get a better job? Would you like to learn more about changing careers or going into business for yourself? Pick at least three topics that are a priority for you. This will also help group members decide who should lead the various meetings. (If you have an interest or expertise in a particular subject, it would make sense for you to lead the meeting that focuses on that topic.)

4. Bank statements, credit-card statements, paycheck stubs, investment-account information, and a list of your monthly obligations like rent, utilities, credit-card or car payments, gym-membership fees, cell-phone bills, etc. This information will provide a snapshot of your financial picture and a good foundation on which to build the discussions at the first meeting. You may decide not to delve into all the details of your finances at the very first meeting, but it's a good idea to have these documents on hand.

Sample Agenda for Meeting #1

Welcome and introductions: Each member should take a few minutes to introduce herself, describe her financial situation in general terms, and explain why she decided to join the group.

Set goals: This is an opportunity for each member to share her personal goals and her collective goals for the group. It is important that you decide early on what you want to get out of the money group and what individual and common goals you are all working toward. (Your goals may change along the way, but it's good to have a clear idea of what's important to you.) Even in the first meeting, you can begin to make a habit of setting short-term goals that can be accomplished between meetings. These can range from trying to live on $20 less a week to calling your credit-card issuers to negotiate a lower rate to taking the time to identify and prioritize your long-term goals in your notebook. You should also discuss long-term goals that may require months or even years, like paying off all your credit-card debt, starting your own business, or buying your dream house. At each meeting, you can check in with one another to see if you were able to accomplish the short-term goals and to talk about any progress made toward achieving your long-term goals. We recommend writing down and posting your goals in a place that is clear and visible to you on a daily basis and bringing a list of them to each meeting.

Share expectations, contributions, and interests: Each member brings her own set of skills and experiences as well as expectations for herself and for the group. So each of you should discuss how you want to contribute to the group's goals and to help other members and what you hope to get in return. For example, as a social worker, Robyn had the experience and expertise to help each of us explore the emotional or psychological reasons for our spending patterns. Katie had once worked for a high-net-worth investor who wrote a regular newsletter, and she was already expanding her own stock portfolio, so she had more experience with investing in the stock market than the rest of us did and was happy to share some of her insights. Each member may also have particular interests. Maybe one of you would prefer to do research on buying real estate in the area, while another is interested in interviewing women who have started their own businesses. Finding out what each person's particular strengths and interests are will help as you assign specific upcoming meeting topics, assignments, and responsibilities to various members.

Decide on your agenda: Consistency is an important part of your money group. Developing a regular agenda will help you get the most out of each meeting. (We've included ours later in this chapter.)

Establish ground rules for the group: Your group needs to discuss and set some parameters on its style or tone. It's important to make sure each member commits to being respectful of the others' comments and opinions, even if she doesn't share them, and to keep the financial information discussed at the meetings confidential (unless all of you agree otherwise).

Come up with a mission statement and name and motto for the group: Want some inspiration? Here's what we came up with at our first meeting. Our motto: Be smart, be rich, be fabulous. Our mission statement: To educate, empower, and inspire members of the Smart Cookies community to take control of their finances and live their richest lives. (We hope we've done that with this book!)

Pick topics to discuss at upcoming meetings: Appoint members to be in charge of the various upcoming topics. They can research the topic beforehand and present their findings for discussion at the meetings. If you're not sure where to start, use the discussion questions from this book.

Decide on an assignment for each member for the next meeting: If you choose not to share the details of your finances at the first meeting, this is a good assignment for the second: Go through your paycheck stubs, bank statements, bills, and other financial documents to determine how much you earn, owe, spend, and save or invest on average each month. Other assignments are usually tied to short-term goals or to researching a particular topic. It's your choice. We encourage you to use the chapter summaries in this book as a guide for money-group assignments and meeting topics.

Decide who will be in charge of various responsibilities for the next meeting: Who will host, take the minutes, bring refreshments, or lead the discussion? Note: We generally ask that the host of the upcoming meeting also be in charge of phoning, e-mailing, or texting members to confirm time and location and any other necessary information (like who is bringing food and drinks).

Final word: This is a chance for members to share any last thoughts or questions before the meeting is adjourned. This doesn't have to be limited to the meeting topic of the day. One great benefit about the group is that you can share your resources with one another in *many* different areas. If you're having a party, for example, you might be able to borrow another group member's serving platter instead of buying one. Or if your car is making funny noises, you can ask other group members for recommendations for a good mechanic. This is also a good time to recognize one another's achievements and acknowledge the commitment that you're each making by being there.

If you need some help coming up with an agenda, here's the general format that we use for each meeting:

1.   Welcome (social time). We always allow ourselves a little time at the beginning of each meeting to talk about non-money-related topics and to catch up with one another before we get down to business.

2. Good News/ Biggest Accomplishments. We like to start each meeting on a positive note, so we have each member talk about her biggest accomplishment since the last meeting. This is also a chance to review the short-term goals from the last meeting, to acknowledge each member who achieved her goal, and to celebrate each member's progress on her long-term goals.

3. Spending Check. Members check in with one another on how well they stuck to their spending plans. If you have not yet set up spending plans, members can speak generally about how they feel about their spending habits since the last meeting. This is a chance for members to confess their splurges and slipups and discuss how to get back on track.

4. Paying Down Debt. Members who have debt talk about the specific steps they've taken to decrease their debt and to avoid taking on more debt and get a chance to celebrate the fact that they are closer to being debt-free.

5. Making More Money. Members can brainstorm and discuss their latest ideas for earning extra income. They can also talk about steps they've taken to increase their salary or to find a better-paying job.

6. Discussion Topic. We also like to share information on particular topics that we've selected for each meeting and to pick new areas of interest to research for the next meeting. All members can research the same topic or one person with a particular interest can research it and then report back at the next meeting. Topics can range from finding the best cell-phone plan to locating consignment stores in the area to researching a particular stock or sector of the market.

7. Goal Setting. Set specific goals and assignments for the next meeting. You can use the exercises at the end of each chapter.

Whatever format works for your group is the one you should use. But remember that you can make changes and adaptations as you go along. In fact, it's often a good idea to do something creative and different at a meeting to keep things interesting, like: celebrating each member's birthday and giving a thoughtful and inexpensive gift from the group, hosting a holiday party at which each member draws the name of another and makes or buys her a gift (we usually set a limit per gift, like $20), or getting together to volunteer with your favorite charity.

However you choose to structure your meetings, we urge you to use this book to help you as you develop agendas and work toward your personal and collective goals. Each chapter summary can be a starting-off point for your meetings. In fact, it's possible that you'll spend an entire meeting on just one question or exercise. We have. Don't try to cram too much into each meeting. These meetings should be a time for you to relax and to enjoy the company and support of your fellow money-group members. It's a chance to vent your frustrations, share your concerns, and celebrate your accomplishments. Money groups are a great way to help you achieve your financial goals, but they're also an opportunity to build lasting friendships. All of us have such busy lives that it's nice to have an excuse to see some of our close friends each week or each month (however often you schedule your meetings). If you're like us, you'll find yourself eagerly anticipating the next meeting—even if it means confessing a recent splurge or admitting your ignorance about a particular financial topic. Don't forget: You're among friends here.

Even after you finish this book, we hope you'll keep it on hand as a resource. You can also log on to our website (www.smartcookies.com) to locate a money group in your area, chat with other women going through similar experiences, share your success stories, check out more of our tips, and download additional work sheets. Join the growing community of Smart Cookies around the world who are committed to being financially successful for life.

Afterword:
Live Your Richest Life

On that Tuesday night in early March 2006, when our first official meeting was called to order, none of us could have imagined that our decision to form this money group would profoundly change the course of our lives. We just knew we needed to improve our finances, and we welcomed the chance to do it with other like-minded women who were committed to the same goals.

It didn't take us long, though, to realize that a money group is not just about money. Not only has it helped us to improve our finances but it's enriched our lives and empowered us to reach goals we might not have on our own. And as friends and colleagues began to see the evidence of our accomplishments, they started asking us how we did it—and if they could join. (Some of them had expressed interest in the idea initially when a couple of us started discussing the possibility of forming a money group. But only the five of us were ready to make the commitment we felt was required at that time.)

Still, we didn't fully realize the potential impact our experience could have on others until we submitted our story to *The Oprah Winfrey Show* website and received an invitation to appear on the show. As we described on air our various financial accomplishments and the nonmonetary benefits we'd gotten from our money group—like friendship, support, and inspiration—we began to understand how sharing our stories, insights, and experience could help others like us. We knew that we couldn't be the only smart, fabulous, and financially completely out-of-control women out there!

After the *Oprah* show taping, Jean Chatzky, a personal-finance writer we greatly admired and were thrilled to meet during the show, asked if we wanted to chat with her on the Oprah & Friends satellite-radio channel that afternoon. When we were live on the air with her, Jean encouraged us to think about writing a book that would offer more details about our money group and explain exactly how we had each been able to achieve our major financial accomplishments over the previous year. That set the wheels in motion. (When the universe comes knocking with an opportunity to live out your wildest dreams with four of your best friends, you don't ignore it!) On the plane ride home from Chicago, we started bouncing ideas off one another and then, when we arrived at home, we discussed the idea with friends and family.

Appearing on *The Oprah Winfrey Show* also gave us a chance to meet another role model of ours, David Bach, whose inspiring book *Smart Women Finish Rich* was a real resource for us in early meetings. The book title also helped give us an idea for our money group's name.

The more we shared with people—regardless of how educated they were or how successful they appeared—the more they wanted to know: How did we do it? What were the most important lessons we learned? Did they need to join a money group or could they do this on their own? They wanted advice on everything from buying real estate to paying off debt to saving for weddings and retirement.

We started with a basic website and an e-mail address (info@smart cookies.com), through which we received hundreds of e-mails in just a few months from people who'd seen us on TV or read about us online or in the paper. Most people who contacted us asked: How could they do what we did? Soon we became a full-fledged business. We hired a fantastic manager to help us explore various avenues to get our message out, and we worked with a web designer to create a site that is user-friendly and full of great information. (We think so, anyway. See for yourself at: smartcookies.com.)

We then had the incredibly good fortune of being connected with Jean's literary agent, who in turn put us in touch with Jennifer Barrett, a talented, bright, and fabulous writer. We clicked right away. Next we partnered with an award-winning production company to create a TV show named—what else?—*Smart Cookies*. Each week we have the chance to help out singles, couples, or families who are in need of a serious money makeover. (Done in a fun way, of course! As you know from our book, our approach is not about lectures, guilt, or deprivation.) We also developed a seminar—one we're proud to say is not your average financial seminar.

Throughout this amazing, unexpected journey that our lives have taken since 2006, our genuine love and respect for one another continue to grow. We are fiercely loyal to one another, to the business, and to our mission to educate, empower, and inspire people all over the world to live their richest lives.

If you have women you're close to in your life, forming a money group will only make your friendships that much stronger. And if you want to meet or connect with other women who are doing this on their own, our website is a good place to start.

Even now, as we work to build our business while fulfilling our other responsibilities, we continue to hold our money-group meetings to check in on our personal progress, share new information or lessons we've learned, and provide support and accountability for one another. The difference is that now we have the opportunity to inspire not just one another but women around the world to live the life they desire. We don't take this opportunity lightly.

We hope that you will use the experiences and the advice we have shared in this book to create the best possible life for yourself. And we encourage you to share your stories and your insights with us and with others like you through our website. You deserve to be financially successful. You deserve to get paid what you are worth and to live your richest life in every sense of the word. We hope you'll take us along on your exciting journey!

Notes

Chapter 1
Page 9 "For all the money single men spend on . . .": U.S. Department of Labor, Bureau of Labor Statistics' Consumer Expenditure Survey, 2005–2006. Tables 43 and 44 at: ftp://ftp.bls.gov/pub/special.requests/ce/crosstabs/y0506/sexbyinc/malesinc. txt, ftp://ftp.bls.gov/pub/special.requests/ce/crosstabs/y0506/sexbyinc/ femalinc.txt.

Page 10 "In 2006, single women, on average, spent more . . .": ibid.

Page 11 "There's no doubt that many women were nodding sympathetically, or cringing, during the episode in which Carrie learns . . .": *Sex and the City*, Episode 64: "Ring a Ding Ding." Accessed at: http://www.hbo.com/city/episode/season4/ episode64.shtml.

Chapter 2
Page 47 "Real median income for those under 35 . . .": "Historical Income Tables— Households" Table H-10, Age of Head of Household: All Races by Median and Mean Income: 1967 to 2006. U.S. Census Bureau: http://www.census.gov/ hhes/www/income/histinc/h10ar.html.

Chapter 4
Page 75 "For the first time since the Great Depression, the Commerce Department reported . . .": U.S. Department of Commerce, Bureau of Economic Analysis. "Personal Income and Outlays: December 2006," released February 1, 2007, at: http://www.bea.gov/newsreleases/national/pi/2007/pi1206.htm.

Page 75 "According to Federal Reserve Board data, the average U.S. cardholder has five credit cards . . .": "Report to the Congress on the Profitability of Credit Card Operations of Depository Institutions," The Federal Reserve Board, June 2006, at: http://federalreserve.gov/boarddocs/rptcongress/creditcard/2006/default.htm.

Page 77 "There's a reason why personal bankruptcies hit an all-time high . . .": "Personal Bankruptcies Hit Record High," CNNMoney.com, January 11, 2006, at: http://money.cnn.com/2006/01/11/pf/personal_bankruptcy/index.htm.

Page 77 ". . . and why nearly half of U.S. households carry a credit-card balance—on average about $5,100, according to the Federal Reserve Board's 2004 Survey of Consumer Finances": Brian K. Bucks, Arthur B. Kennickell, and Kevin B. Moore, "Recent Changes in U.S. Family Finances: Evidence from the 2001 and 2004 Survey of Consumer Finances," Federal Reserve Board's Division of Research and Statistics: http://www.federalreserve.gov/pubs/oss/oss2/2004/bull0206.pdf.

Page 77 "Others claim the number is even higher—CardWeb.com, which tracks credit-card trends, says the average credit-card debt among households with at least one credit card was more than $8,900 in 2002": "Credit Card Debt: 3/13/03" at: http://www.cardweb.com/cardtrak/news/2003/march/13a.html.

Page 77 "By this spring, total U.S. consumer debt had soared to nearly $2.56 trillion . . ." "Consumer Credit," Federal Reserve Statistical Release, May 7, 2008, at http://www.federalreserve.gov/releases/g19/20080507/.

Page 77 "Not only are we more likely to go bankrupt . . .": Gardner, Marilyn, "Bankruptcy Reform Hits Women Hard," the *Christian Science Monitor*, April 4, 2005, at: http://www.csmonitor.com/2005/0404/p13s01-wmgn.html.

Page 77 "The U.S. budget deficit hit an all-time high in 2004 of $413 billion—or about $1,400 *per person* living in America . . .": "Resident Population Projections: 50 2004 to 20," U.S. Census Bureau Statistical Abstract of the United States. 2004–, at: http://www.census.gov/prod/2004pubs/04statab/pop.pdf.

Page 77 "It has since declined, but not by much: It was expected to be about $396 billion . . .": "U.S. CBO forecasts $396 bln FY08 budget deficit," Reuters, March 6, 2008, at: http://www.reuters.com/article/economicNews/idUSNO626239720080306.

Page 77 "When President Bush announced the rebates . . .": "President Bush Discusses Economy," transcript, The White House, Office of the Press Secretary, March 7, 2008, at: http://www.whitehouse.gov/news/releases/2008/03/20080307-4.html.

Page 77 "Consumer spending does account for nearly 70 percent of the country's

Gross Domestic Product": "Facts on Policy: Consumer Spending," Hoover Institution, December 19, 2006, at: http://www.hoover.org/research/factson policy/facts/4931661.html.

Page 78 "The volume of debit-card transactions in the U.S. has more than tripled since 2000 . . .": Appoorva, Saxena, "Debit Card Usage Surpasses Credit Cards in 2006," CreditUnions.com, January 1, 2007, at: http://www.creditunions. com/home/articles/template.asp?article_id=2183.

Page 79 ". . . mainly because they're charged processing fees each time customers use their debit or credit cards . . .": Jeffrey, Simon, "Merchants encourage use of PINs for debit card payments," Creditcards.com, May 14, 2007, at: http://www.credit cards.com/Merchants-Encourage-PIN-Usage.php.

Chapter Five

Page 111 "Foreclosure filings were up 75 percent in 2007 from the year before . . .": "U.S. Foreclosure activity up 75 percent in 2007," RealtyTrac, January 29, 2008, at: http://www.realtytrac.com/ContentManagement/pressrelease.aspx? ChannelID=9&ItemID=4303&accnt=64847.

Page 116 "One-third of all U.S. credit-card holders are now paying interest rates of 20 percent or more . . .": Wheary, Jennifer, and Tamara Draut, "Who Pays? The Winners and Losers of Credit Card Deregulation," August 1,2007, at: http://demos.org/pub1463.cfm.

Page 116 "That same year, more than one-third of all active credit-card accounts in the country were assessed a late fee at least once . . .": "Credit Cards: Increased Complexity in Rates and Fees Heightens Need for More Effective Disclosures to Consumers," U.S. Government Accountability Office, September 2006, at: http://www.gao.gov/new.items/d06929.pdf.

Chapter Six

Page 137 "Women working full-time still earn, on average, about 80 cents for every dollar earned by men in the United States . . .": "Median usual weekly earnings of full-time wage and salary workers by detailed occupation and sex," Table 18, U.S. Bureau of Labor Statistics at: http://www.bls.gov/cps/wlf-table18-2005.pdf.

Page 137 "The good news is that's up from 63 cents in 1979 . . .": "Highlights of Women's Earnings of 2006," U.S. Bureau of Labor Statistics, September 2007, Report 1000, at: http://www.bls.gov/cps/cpswom2006.pdf.

Chapter Seven

Page 161 "Be aware that banks may automatically roll your CD into a new one if you don't notify them not to do so . . .": "Answers & Solutions for Customers of National Banks: Answers About CDs and Certificates of Deposit," U.S. Department of Treasury, Comptroller of the Currency Administrator of National Banks, at: http://www.helpwithmybank.gov/faqs/banking_cd.html.

Chapter Eight

Page 177 "Sales of existing homes in the U.S. were down 22 percent and prices of existing homes were down 6 percent between the end of 2006 and the end of 2007 . . .": "Existing-home Sales Down in December but 2007 was Fifth Highest on Record," National Realtors Association, January 24, 2008, at: http://www.realtor.org/press_room/news_releases/2008/ehs_jan08_existing_home _sales_down.html.

Page 178 "Over the long run, you can generally expect the value of your home to go up . . .": "U.S. Economic Outlook," National Realtors Association, April 2008, at: http://www.realtor.org/Research.nsf/files/CurrentForecast.pdf/$FILE/Current Forecast.pdf.

Page 178 "As long as you've owned the home and lived in it for a minimum of two years, you can exclude $250,000 of profit . . .": "IRS Issues Home Sales Exclusion Rules," IR-2002-142, Internal Revenue Service, December 23, 2002, at: http://www.irs.gov/newsroom/article/0,,id=105042,00.html.

Page 180 "That's because most lenders don't want your total monthly obligations . . . (the Federal Housing Administration's threshold is a little higher, at 41 percent).": "100 Questions & Answers About Buying a New Home," Homes & Communities, U.S. Department of Housing and Urban Development, at: http://www .hud.gov/offices/hsg/sfh/buying/buyhm.cfm.

Page 181 "In 2007, the average closing and related costs for someone getting a $200,000 mortgage loan in Indianapolis were about $2,339, but someone in New York City . . .": Holden, Lewis, "New York has costliest mortgage fees," Bankrate.com, July 12, 2007, at: http://www.bankrate.com/brm/news/ mortgages/2007/closing_costs_overview_1.asp.

Page 183 "Many banks will allow you to put down less than that on a home, but if you do so, your lender will likely require you to purchase private mortgage insurance (or PMI) . . .": "Private Mortgage Insurance," Consumer Affairs and Public Information staff, Federal Reserve Bank of San Francisco brochure, at: http://www.frbsf.org/publications/consumer/pmi.html#what.

Page 184 "By February 2008, the average price of a single-family home in the U.S.

had fallen to $241,900, down nearly 12.5 percent from the previous summer . . .": "Existing Home Sales," National Association of Realtors, 2008, at: http://www.realtor.org/Research.nsf/files/EHSreport.pdf/$FILE/EHSreport.pdf.

Page 184 "The median sale price of an existing single-family home in Las Vegas, once one of the nation's fastest-growing cities, fell nearly 13 percent between the end of 2006 and the end of 2007 . . .": "Median Sales Price of Existing Single-Family Homes for Metropolitan Areas," National Association of Realtors, 2008, at: http://www.realtor.org/Research.nsf/files/MSAPRICESF.pdf/$FILE/MSAPRICESF.pdf.

Page 190 "In addition to being licensed to sell real estate, realtors must belong to the National Association of Realtors and pledge to abide by its code of ethics . . .": "NAR: Real Estate Resources: 2008 Code of Ethics and Standards of Practice," National Association of Realtors, January 1, 2008, at: http://www.realtor.org/mempolweb.nsf/pages/code.

Resources

Introduction
For more information on Oprah's Debt Diet, check out: www.oprah.com/
money/debtdiet/money_debtdiet_main.jhtml.

Chapter 3
For help with perfect-day exercise estimates for . . .
- A baby: Several sites offer checklists of what you'll need for a baby, including: www.surebaby.com/baby_checklist.php, www.expectantmothers guide.com, and www.babycenter.com. You can estimate prices by checking retailers with online sites like Target, Wal-Mart, Buy Buy Baby, and Babies R Us.
- A car: Sites that offer information on car values include Kelley Blue Book (kbb.com), www.autotrader.com, or *Consumer Reports* (www.consumer reports.org/cro/cars/index.htm).
- A home: Check with a local realtor or check home prices on www .craigslist.org, www.trulia.com, or www.zillow.com, among others.

Chapter 4
Need more information on some of those tips we offered to cut back a little without lowering your standard of living?
- Exercise with friends: Get more information on YMCA rates and locations at: http://www.ymca.net.

- Wrinkle creams: Learn more about the *Consumer Reports* study of wrinkle creams at: http://www.consumerreports.org/health/healthy-living/beauty-personal-care/cosmetics/wrinkle-creams/wrinkle-creams-1-07/overview/0107_cream_ov_1.htm.
- Internet phone service (or VoIP): Go to NextAdvisor.com for a comparison of different VoIP services.
- Be energy-efficient: For more tips on saving energy at home and at work, go to: http://www.energysavers.gov.

Donate and deduct:

- Need help estimating the value of a donation? The Salvation Army has a good value guide online at: http://www.satruck.com/ValueGuide .aspx.
- To find a drop-off center near you, plug your zip code into this site: http://www.satruck.com/FindDropoff.aspx.
- To find a Goodwill Industries center near you, go to: http://locator .goodwill.org.
- Some Big Brothers Big Sisters facilities accept donations of clothing, furniture, office supplies, exercise equipment, or cars. To find a Big Brothers Big Sisters agency near you, go to: http://www.bbbs.org/site/c.diJKKYPLJvH/b.1690505/k.EC31/Find_a_Local_Agency.htm.
- For more information on Soles4Souls, go to: http://www.soles4souls.org.

Chapter 5
Education loans:

- For more information on federal Pell Grants, go to: http://www.ed.gov/programs/fpg/index.html.
- To learn more about Stafford federal student loans, go to: http://www.staffordloan.com.
- For more on the Newcombe Scholarship for Mature Women, check out: www.newcombefoundation.org.
- To search various scholarships and aid available for higher education, try these sites: Finaid.org, collegeboard.com, and scholarships.com.

Business loans and resources:

- Check out the Small Business Administration for available aid and other resources: sba.gov.
- For more information on women's groups like Ladies Who Launch, Count

Me In, and the Forum for Women Entrepreneurs and Executives, go to ladieswholaunch.com, countmein.org, or fwe.org.

Buying a car:
- Check *Consumer Reports* (consumerreports.org) or Kelley Blue Book (kbb.com) for more ratings and research on specific models and the best resale values.
- For the best deal, try buying directly from the car owner, through classified ads or craigslist.org.

Trimming transportation costs:
- For more information on the car sharing service called Zipcar, go to: zipcar.com.
- If you have a car and live in New York, Boston, Washington, D.C., or Philadelphia, check out bestparking.com for the best daily and monthly garage rates.
- If you're in a major city, you can save money on cab fare by visiting Rideamigos.com, which lets you link up with others in your neighborhood who are looking for a cab to popular locations.

Credit-card calculator:
- Want to see how long it will take you to pay off your credit-card balance— and how much interest you'll pay—if you make just the minimum payment each month? Go to: http://www.bankrate.com/brm/calc/MinPayment.asp.
- Want to see what it will take to pay off your credit-card balance by a certain date? Go to: http://www.bankrate.com/brm/calc/creditcardpay.asp.

Credit-card holders bill of rights:
- To read the text of the bill introduced by Rep. Carolyn Maloney, go to: http://maloney.house.gov/documents/financial/h.r.5244billtext.pdf.
- To see where the bill stands, plug the bill number (H.R. 5244) into the home page at http://thomas.loc.gov/.

Consumer credit counseling:
- Try calling your creditors directly first.
- If that doesn't work, look for accredited, licensed organizations with certi-fied credit counselors.
- Try the National Foundation for Credit Counselors at nfcc.org or the Association

of Independent Consumer Credit Counseling Agencies at AICCCA.org or Consolidated Credit Counseling Services, Inc., at consolidatedcredit.org.

Getting your credit report and credit score:
- You're entitled to one free copy of your credit report each year from each of the three major credit bureaus, though they're not required to provide your score. Only one website is authorized to fill orders for the free annual credit report: www.annualcreditreport.com.
- Get your scores directly from the three major credit bureaus: (equifax.com), Experian (Experian.com), or TransUnion (transunion.com).

Chapter 6

Find out what you're worth:
- Payscale.com offers a free salary-comparison report for your job in your city, based on your experience and education, using information from other anonymous users.
- You can also get salary information for jobs by logging on to sites like salary.com, workopolis.com, or monster.com, or go to bls.gov.

Test-drive your dream job:
- You can book a trip and spend a day or more working in your dream job through vocationvacations.com.
- Another option is to apply for a formal apprenticeship, a combination of on-the-job training and related instruction. For more information, go to: http://www.dol.gov/dol/topic/training/apprenticeship.htm.
- To find an apprenticeship program in one of a dozen industries dubbed "high growth" by the government, go to: http://www.careervoyages.gov/apprenticeship-main.cfm.

Earn extra cash:
- Marketing stock photos can be a convenient way for you to build up a secondary income stream. Try Fotolia, Dreamstime, Shutterstock, and Big Stock Photo to upload and market your photos.
- Use craigslist.org to rent your parking space or sell old clothes or other items.
- Rent your home for use as a location for commercials, TV shows, or movies. You can register your home directly with film studios, production companies, and advertising firms, which maintain lists of properties available for shooting. Check out eHow.com for tips, or *Opening Your Door to Hollywood*, a 2006 book by producer James Perry.

- Be an extra. You don't need a Screen Actors Guild (SAG) membership or even any acting experience to qualify—just the patience to sit on a set for hours and the flexibility to try out a lot of different costumes and lines. Pay can range from $100 to more than $1,000 a day. Check out sites like www.extratalentagency.com.
- Help friends find better jobs. Internet sites like H3.com and jobthread.com connect employers with prospective employees, many of whom are already employed and not actively job-hunting, via networking. The rewards for referring a candidate who gets hired range from a few hundred dollars to as much as $5,000.
- Be a secret shopper. Check out sites like www.nationalassociationofmystery shoppers.org or www.mysteryshoppersamerica.com for more information. (Just note that they each require membership fees—starting at $24.95 and $34 respectively as of early 2008—to gain access to training and potential jobs.)

Chapter 7
Checking out investments:

Stocks, bonds, mutual funds, and exchange-traded funds (ETFs): If you're looking for information and ratings on bonds issued by a particular company or governmental entity, search the rating agencies' websites: moodys.com, standard andpoors.com, fitchibca.com, ambest.com, or dbrs.com. If you've got a few mutual funds or ETFs in mind and want to know how the fees and related expenses could affect your return, the Financial Industry Regulatory Authority (FINRA) website offers a tool that compares the expenses of up to three of the more than 18,000 mutual funds or exchange-traded funds in its database at: http://apps.finra.org/investor_information/ea/1/mfetf.aspx. Need some help deciding on a fund? A good place to start is a website like Morningstar.com, which offers ratings and nonbiased general information on a range of funds. You can also check out Yahoo! Finance or other personal finance sites to find some of the best fund and individual stock performers in particular categories.

Online investing: Several sites offer rankings and information on online brokerages, including:
- Bankrate.com (http://www.bankrate.com/brm/news/pf/20001211c.asp).
- J.D. Power & Associates (http://www.jdpower.com/finance/ratings/ online_investment/index.asp).
- Kiplinger's Personal Finance (at http://articles.moneycentral.msn.com/ Investing/Extra/TheBestOnlineBrokers.aspx).

- Smart Money (http://www.smartmoney.com/brokers/index.cfm?story= august2007).

Chapter 8
Buying a home:
- For more information on FHA loans and tips for buying a home, check out HUD's "100 Questions and Answers About Buying a New Home" at http://www.hud.gov/offices/hsg/sfh/buying/buyhm.cfm.
- Compare mortgage rates and calculate mortgage payments at bankrate.com.

Researching home prices:
- Every quarter, the National Association of Realtors publishes median prices for single-family homes in nearly 150 of the nation's biggest metro areas on its site: www.realtor.org.
- You can also check the federal government's Office of Federal Housing Enterprise Oversight's House Price Index, which includes separate house price indexes for several major metropolitan areas (http://www.ofheo .gov/hpi.aspx) that reveal overall trends in housing prices.

Finding foreclosed properties:
- Foreclosed properties can be found in many neighborhoods at below-market prices, since the owners often are desperate to sell and are looking to get whatever they can for their homes.
- You can check your local paper. The Department of Housing and Urban Development (www.hud.gov), Fannie Mae (www.fanniemae.com), and Freddie Mac (www.freddiemac.com) also all have links to listings of foreclosed properties.

Index